# Sex and the Narcissist

By

H G Tudor

All Rights Reserved

Copyright 2016

# Sex and the Narcissist

## By

## HG Tudor

All rights reserved. No part of this book may be reproduced, stored in a retrieval system, or transmitted in any form or by any means, electronic, mechanical, photocopying, recording, or otherwise, without the express written permission of the publisher.

Published by Insight Books

# Contents

1. Introduction
2. How Do We Regard Sex?
3. What Are We Thinking During Sex?
4. The Type of Sexual Narcissist
5. Why Are We So Good At Sex?
6. The Sexual Identity
7. The Seduction Stage
8. The Role of Sex in the Seduction Stage
9. Why Are You Addicted to Our Sex?
10. Sex in the Devaluation Stage
11. Sex and Hoovering
12. Conclusion

# Introduction

Sex is not the answer. Sex is the question. Yes is the answer. Sex is all pervading. At its most fundamental level it is a tool for procreation. It is the method by which the human race keeps on growing. It is, to most, a pleasant experience. It occupies the minds of many, many people. How do they get sex? How do they get more sex? What can they use sex for? People like to look and feel sexy. As the saying goes, sex sells. Sex is everywhere. Turn off the safe search filter on whichever internet search engine you use and type in anything, any word or phrase that springs into your mind. I daresay that amidst the images that your results turns up there will be sexual images amongst them. Only the other day I searched for a boxing bell. There amongst the many images of said bells was a topless woman wearing boxing gloves. Sexual imagery is rife. Our pop stars cavort on stage wearing next to nothing and engage in highly charged choreographed erotic dances. From Elvis the Pelvis, through to Britney and Madonna's pseudo-lesbian embrace and then onto Miley Cyrus and her naked wrecking ball antics. Erotic novels enjoyed a somewhat dubious resurgence thanks to the puzzlingly popular Fifty Shades of Grey. The online content of once fastidious newspapers will contain pictures of some celebrity on a beach or wearing a skimpy outfit at an awards ceremony. Once average-looking people become super sexy thanks to the magical power of sympathetic lighting and the airbrush in order to appear more attractive, more alluring and sexier. Everywhere you go sex is in your face. From the attractive underwear, you put on first thing in the morning, the advertisements in between your breakfast television, and the breathy ads on the radio as you drive to work and not forgetting the posters on bus shelters, buildings and massive city centre screens. Books, television, music, perfume, cars, films and so much more offer sex. Even a well-known British retailer created advertisements to sell its food range, which were dubbed as 'food porn'. All of this is dominated by the internet which channels sex right into your face through a thousand different websites all dedicated to porn. From the vanilla variety through to the kinky and onto the disturbed, every sexual taste and preference is now catered for. We are surrounded by sex.

Sex however is at its most potent and most important in the context of a relationship. Sex is regarded as an integral part of a relationship between two people whether heterosexual, homosexual or transgender. Sex creates a significant bond between those people who are in a couple. It is the basis of discussion and arguments. Too much sex? Too little sex? Sex outside the relationship? Involving a third party in the sexual union? Sex is a complex dynamic. The importance of sex is no different yet is entirely different in my world, the world of the narcissist. Sex is important to my kind and me. We regard it, just as most people do, as a fundamental part of a relationship. The purpose and role of sex is vastly different however to a narcissist. Sex serves one massive purpose and that is to harvest fuel. Fuel is the central purpose of the narcissistic existence. We must have this fuel, we need this fuel and we engage in a ceaseless quest to acquire it. Sex provides us with a fantastic instrument to assist us in this mission to gather fuel. If we do not have fuel, we will be consigned to oblivion.

Acquiring it therefore takes on an unequalled level of importance. Sex provides us with a highly effective method of getting this fuel.

Our fuel comes in two types. Positive fuel from when we receive love, attention, adoration and admiration. Negative fuel from the emotional reactions of fear, anger, frustration, sadness and so much more. Sex enables us to gather both positive and negative fuel. We deploy a wide range of manipulative techniques in order to harvest this fuel and sex ranks as one of the most powerful methods of doing so. It is so powerful because to our victims, our sweet empathic victims, sex invariably is equated to love and therefore it has a huge emotional impact. Your attitude towards sex enables us to use it to further our hunt for fuel. Accordingly, at the heart of everything we say and do that is associated with sex, fuel is at the heart of it. It shapes our attitudes, frames our beliefs and drives our behaviour. The relationship with a narcissist is tumultuous, euphoric and despairing and the sexual relationship is no different. Why do we use sex as we do? Why do our sexual appetites and preferences change? Why do we engage in certain sexual behaviours? Probably more than any other element of the relationship with a narcissist, sex is the one that raises so many questions. Now you are going to get the answers.

I will take you into the depths of my narcissistic mind and share with you the secrets of the narcissist and sex. I will not pull any punches, this is a very adult topic and we are all adults, although we will not slip into the gratuitous. My observations will be direct, graphic and at times uncomfortable but by reading how I regard sex you will gain a huge understanding of why the narcissist behaves as he does and this will benefit you. Through understanding, you will be better able to protect yourself. Through understanding, you will be able to make sense of what once seemed unfathomable. You will be appalled yet enlightened. You will recognise much that is applicable to you and your experiences and now in an undiluted form straight from the mind of a narcissist you will begin to understand. You will learn why sex is used in the way it is by us, why it is so important and why we behave as we do. You will gain an insight into the twisted thought process behind our actions and you will understand what drives us. Most of all you will learn that sex is not about sex to us. It is about something far more important. I have utilised my considerable experiences, the behaviour of other narcissists that I know and as ever I have been assisted in gaining an understanding of our behaviours and their context from Dr E and Dr O.

I began this introduction explaining how all-pervading sex is. Sex is all around us yet the role of sex to you is far different from its role to us. As Oscar Wide succinctly put it

"Everything in the world is about sex except sex. Sex is about power."

Read on and understand why power matters to the narcissist in the sexual arena.

# How Do We Regard Sex?

Sex is a tool. It is a device. Sex is a very effective mechanism that enables us to obtain that thing which we crave more than anything else; fuel. We do not equate sex and love as being something that goes together. We regard them as entirely separate and not something that we would ever combine. I know a lot about sex or perhaps more accurately, I know a lot about how people like you regard sex. When I mean people like you, I mean our victims. I mean decent, caring, honest and empathic people. You are normal people. You are normal people who regard sex as a healthy element in a strong and loving relationship. You see it as a device for pleasure, you regard it as a means of demonstrating love by being intimate with another person and you consider it a barometer for the state of your relationship. I know that initially you will have a period of time when you enjoy sex regularly with your chosen partner. I know this because I specifically ask those who I have targeted about their sex lives. I do not do so in some crass and intrusive fashion. That is not my style. I will watch a film with you and use what happens in that film between the two leads as a basis for discussion. Take for example the film Wuthering Heights and I am referring to the version from the early 1990s that starred Ralph Fiennes as Heathcliff and Juliette Binoche as Catherine. When Catherine passed away, she is later lying in an open coffin at her home after being married to Edgar. Edgar looks upon her and whilst there is clear affection for her, his repressed upbringing has the effect that he only plants a kiss on Catherine's forehead and then he retreats. Heathcliff soon after this breaks into the grange and seeing Catherine lying there he grabs her, overcome with grief and hauls her partially from the coffin, holding her close and burying his face next to hers as he cries. His passion for Catherine has been undiminished. I may remark to the intimate partner with whom I have watched the film about how Heathcliff's passion was such a contrast to Edgar's far more refined behaviour and I will ask whether she thinks it is possible to sustain such a passion for such a time just for one person. I have asked this question on several occasions and I am met with answers which whilst phrased differently all amount to the same thing. I am told that early in normal relationships, the passion is there for all to see and it manifests itself especially through regular and energetic sexual congress. After a time this fire dies down. The passion is still there but it becomes something much more deep-seated and substantial. Occasionally it will appear but far less often and alongside this, the sexual side of a relationship diminishes. There is a deep love, a companionship and affection but the sexual element takes on a more substantial side. It becomes more about demonstrating love and commitment, an expression of contentment rather than the spontaneous and firework-laden couplings that had taken place previously. This is not something I have ever experienced. I will expand on this in due course but in general, terms the answers that I receive tell me that in the beginning the sex is exciting, urgent and frequent. It may be experimental with new things tried as boundaries are pushed back. Over time this energy and excitement subsides and gives way to something more meaningful and deeper. This enables me to understand the value that you place on the sexual element of a relationship because these concepts are alien to me. I do not see that initial stage of jumping into bed every day, making love in different places and positions as something that is done because it is exciting and both parties have been caught up in a whirlwind of desire for one another. I regard that initial stage as purely a means to make you addicted to me. The heady passion of the start of a relationship where new journeys are embarked on and fresh discoveries are made about what people enjoy and do not enjoy is not something I recognise. I see it purely as an opportunity to give you what you want so you want me. In the later stages, I do not regard sex as an expression of deep-seated love and commitment to another person. I see it as a device by which I can push and pull you, manipulate and control you in order to make you give me more fuel.

    I know sex is important to you and your kind. I see all of the documentaries and talk shows that have been created to address sexual issues between people. I see the deluge of pornography on the internet. I see the pop stars gyrating, the film stars wearing next to nothing on the red carpet and how sex features in film, television, books and plays because you regard it as so important. I know from my observations and discussions that you consider it to be important because it makes you feel loved, it allows you to show love, it makes you feel good, it makes you excited, it makes you content and it makes you feel wanted. I agree it is important but I only see it as important because it provides me with fuel. I have no interest in becoming excited by it. I might be excited at the prospect of the delicious positive fuel that you provide to me as you praise my masterful technique between the sheets. I do not need to feel wanted. I want you to want me because then I can keep extracting fuel from you and what better device is there to bind you to me than sex? You place great stock in this expression of intimacy. In your world, the fact that you have to be together, make love and then look longingly at one another satisfies so many needs that you have. Much of this you have been conditioned to expect. You have been shaped by society to have a pre-conceived notion of what love is and moreover how sex shapes that love. A classic example is fiction's obsession with the synchronised orgasm. I have had many sexual partners and in all the times, I have coupled with them there has never been an occasion where we have both come together. Never. Yet, the makers of films, the writers of romance novels will have you believe that this is something that people should try and attain, it is the golden moment of sex. This is just one example of how you have been conditioned to think and behave when it comes to sex and love, because most of the time, people like you, entwine those two things together. Even when you might be taken roughly form behind in the kitchen, splayed over the counter and the act is short, harsh and all about the man satisfying himself you will tell yourself that he loves me because he wants to have me that way. He is still attracted to me. When you fall into one another's arms and have slow sex you tell yourself this is because you are so deeply in love and both of you are entirely wrapped up in one another. You make love in the car in a lay-by because you had the urge. You love one another still because you have this exciting and instantaneous sex. Your kind equate sex as intimacy as love because that is the way that you have been conditioned to think. You have no difficulty with the concept of loving someone through having sex with them, the two things are bound up and we encourage this in our manipulation of you.

In the same way, you have been conditioned to believe in the happy ever after. This is also a method of causing you to regard love in a certain fashion, just in the same way as you have been conditioned to regard sex in a certain fashion.

"I need a knight in shining armour to come and rescue me."

"Where is my Prince Charming?"

These are familiar comments and they all arise because of the myth that has been created and perpetuated. It is well established that my kind and me create an illusion. Have you considered the fact that we are just giving you what you expect? We are saying what you want to hear, doing what you want to see and complying with a pre-conceived notion of how relationships ought to be? How was this idea formulated? Who created the concept of the happy ever after? Was it the Brothers Grimm or Hans Christian Andersen through the fairy tales that they wrote or were they just recording something, which had existed orally for centuries before as they added a new gloss to the fairy tale? Maybe we should blame Hollywood for its depiction of how love conquers all and the hero saves the day by dashing to aid the stereotypical damsel in distress. The number of films in which that happens is numerous. Richard Gere appears in his limousine to woo Julia Roberts in Pretty Woman, in Love Actually; Hugh Grant goes door to door in search of the tea-lady Martine McCutcheon and in The Matrix Trilogy or even the kick-ass feisty Trinity is masterfully caught by Neo to prevent her falling. In Rear Window, James Stewart rescues Grace Kelly, in the unusual Wild at Heart, Nicholas Cage (playing Nicholas Cage) comes to the assistance of Laura Dern at a metal gig and who can forget Shrek where an ogre goes hell for leather to beat Prince Charming of all people and gain the hand of Princess Fiona. I am sure you can think of many more examples. There are thousands of instances of this stylised concept of romance and love. Certain films dedicate the entirety of the production to it. Others have a different subject matter but the concept remains. Luke Skywalker went to rescue the Princess trapped in the Death Star. Clint Eastwood helped the young woman in Pale Rider and she fell in love with him although he left her (was that a cowboy discard perhaps?) and even uber narcissist James Bond gives the Bond Girl her slice of heaven for a few screen minutes. Everywhere you look the idea of romance and the knight in shining armour becomes reinforced. Pop songs, advertisements (once upon a time a man would go to great lengths just to deliver a box of chocolates to his paramour in the Milk Tray ad), greetings cards, magazines, newspapers, sitcoms, novels and so on and so forth. The airbrushed, photo shopped, sweeping sound tracked and every sense heightened message is driven at you each day. There is a dashing hero (or heroine) out there who will save you and treat you like a princess (or prince).

This is the message that is all around you. This is what you have been raised to expect. Someone will save the day and sweep you off your feet. Everything is going to be all right. You will have your happy ever after. It is hardly surprising that you have bought into this master illusion. Who would not? It is all pervading and virtually impossible to resist. It appeals to that deep-seated desire to be cared for and protected and this is done by maintaining a myth that someone should arrive on a white charger, armour gleaming to pull you from the clutches of the evil troll or moustachioed villain.

"I need a hero," sang Bonnie Tyler and then she laid down the criteria required for said hero to attain. I do not recall her mentioning a steady income, being handy with a paintbrush and making a nice cup of tea. Instead, she, along with countless others, generates an ideal and you bought into it. You want the fairy tale. I understand it. Why would you not when all around you, you are being told that this is the way it should be. Who would not want that sensation of being swept off their feet, romanced and made to feel wonderful? Moreover, who says we do not provide it? There is no denying that when our kind come along we invariably pick you up in a marvellous whirlwind of love, attention and affection as we suck you into an illusion. Where does the fault lie? Is it us that are to blame for creating this construct to draw you to us? Is it your fault for falling for the myth and casting common sense aside for wanting the unattainable? Alternatively, does the blame lie elsewhere? Is it those that created and now maintain this illusion? If it is those in this latter category that have created this monster that you believe in and we merely comply with, then the question becomes this. Who are they? Are they your kind or our kind?

I understand all of this. I understand exactly what you have come to expect and in doing so this enables me to adjust my manipulative behaviour to give you exactly what you want. You see sex as the gateway to love and intimacy. That is fine by me. I will go along with that. I do not believe it. I do not feel it, but if it enables me to dupe you so you fall in love with me and spray me with admiring positive fuel then I will buy into this illusion and create it.

Why do I not believe it? Have I not emerged in the same world as you? If this conditioning has taken place and made you regard sex and love in a certain way then why has it not been the same for me? The answer is because I emerged in a completely different world to you. In my world, I regard sex purely as a device. The feelings you attribute to it have been denied to me. I have been stripped of those feelings because they do not serve any purpose for me. I must harvest fuel and therefore I have evolved in the best possible shape to achieve that aim. This means that not all the things you attribute sex with namely enjoyment, pleasure, intimacy and love apply to me. This might cause you to think that since that is the case would I then not remain chaste. Would I not refrain from having sex because it does not generate the same reaction in me as it does in you? That is a valid question. I do however know from listening, watching and questioning what it means to you and therefore I know that sex provides me with an excellent opportunity to use it to ensnare you. I know that by providing you with great sex, passionate sex whereby I say all the things that you have been conditioned to expect then you will fall for me, give me fuel, become addicted to me and never want to let go.

I use sex as a weapon. I use it to trap you. I actually find the whole act mundane. The intimacy you enjoy from it horrifies me because I have no desire to become so close to somebody as it will not serve any purpose. In fact, the suggestion of intimacy troubles me because this suggests opening yourself up to someone else. I cannot do that. I cannot risk taking such a step for the betrayal that will surely come (as it has always come – more on that later) will destroy me. I derive some pleasure from it as I have a physical reaction from the application of a body against mine. This stimulation will evoke a physical reaction in me, which feels pleasant in the same way that masturbation feels pleasant. There is nothing beyond that. When I couple with somebody the sensations I feel are similar to those when I masturbate. You should understand that on a physical level that is all sex feels like to me. I am in effect using somebody else's body parts to masturbate. Your mouth, your hand, your vagina and/or your anus may as well be my hand. It is a mechanical act. The physical sensations I experience when I am inside you are no different to when I take my penis in my hand and stroke it.

If you think there is anything similar to the emotional sensations that you experience when you have sex or as you might prefer it, make love, then you would be wrong. There is no sense of connection with that person, no deep-seated desire, no sense of feeling deeply in love. I am not lifted to a higher plane by this coupling. I do not feel like the rest of the world has melted away leaving only you and I. I do not feel a huge spiritual connection with you. I know about such feelings because this is what you tell me you feel and I am more than content to repeat these sentences to you and other people because this is what you want to hear. I do not feel them however.

There is a physical response to the touching and the caressing and no more. Were it not for the response I obtain from you and the necessity of that response then having sex with another person would be entirely pointless. I may as well masturbate and be done with it if the only thing I obtained from it was a physical release. I do however achieve far more from the sexual act (or the withholding of the same) because I garner fuel, control and power. I know you do not gather these things because you have told me what sex does for you and those words are never mentioned. You get satisfaction, a sense of release, a sense of closeness and intimacy, a sense of feeling good. All entirely different to what I get from sex.

Sex with another person is a mechanical act. I go through the motions, as I would do so were I masturbating. The act is not about acquiring some deep emotional connection between us. It is about me achieving the following:-

- Impressing you with my formidable technique

- Gathering fuel from you from your admiration

- Making you addicted and dependent on me

- Methods of control over you

- Creating something which I can then remove in order to gather fuel

- Creating something which I can then remove in order to control you

We regard sex as a method to further our aims. There are of course other ways of achieving these outcomes but few, if any, are as powerful as sex. If hugging engendered the same result, I would become a world champion hugger. If playing chess with you gave me the same outcomes as sex does then I would be a Grand Master. Do not think that sex is special for us in the same way as it is for you. It is not. It is a tool, a highly effective tool that we will wield in all manner of differing ways in order to get what we want. It is special to us in the sense that it gives us fuel and makes us feel powerful but that it different to what it does for you. You are merely an addition to the process to gather fuel. Perversely enough, I have often been told that when you make love with me you feel like you are merging with me and becoming one. I agree. You are becoming once with me. I am subsuming you because you are my appliance. I have attached you to me and we are becoming one. You supply fuel and I consume it. A perfect match.

# What Are We Thinking?

What is going through our minds when we slip between the sheets with you? What are we really thinking when we take you to bed? Are we thinking the same thoughts as you? Are we delighted in coupling with you, losing ourselves in you, feeling love and feeling loved? Let me enlighten you. I shall describe below a typical sexual encounter between a newly acquired victim and me. I have undertaken my usually preparatory work and begun my seduction of you through a handful of very enjoyable dates. I have said all the right things to make you feel wanted. I have demonstrated an interest in those things, which stimulate you and those, which you hold dear. I have impressed you with my tales of my achievements and I have laid on the flattery by using many tools of seduction from my devilish toolkit. We have left the restaurant and gone to your house. A further drink was forgotten about as I began kissing you at the front door and now you have led me into your bedroom. I am aroused by the physical sensation of engaging in congress with an attractive female but what is actually arousing me is the prospective fuel that will gain from this encounter. Not only that, this coupling will allow me to wrap more of my tendrils around you and exert my seductive control over you to a greater degree. In this typical example of my physical seduction of someone, I will add what is going through my mind in brackets and italics. In bold I shall indicate where the fuel is being gathered.

We are kissing in your bedroom and I hear you make a murmur of satisfaction. (*Good she is enjoying this I had best show her I am as well.*) **FUEL.** I make a noise of pleasure as well which causes you to grip me harder. I move my mouth around to nibble at your neck and bite it lightly. You give another moan of pleasure and tilt your head back. *(Good she likes that, duly noted, let us continue doing that)*. **FUEL.** I continue to lightly bite your neck and move my mouth onto your exposed shoulder as I reach around and slide my hands under your top at the back and allow my nails to scratch gently your back. You press harder against me. (*Excellent, another hit, keep doing that*). **FUEL.** You are unbuttoning my shirt and letting your hands roam over my torso. I lift my mouth from your shoulder and slide off your top. I move my mouth back to yours and kiss you intently. I them move my mouth to your neck again and then up to your ear but you shift slightly (*No, not keen on the ear being licked or nibbled, duly noted, go back to the neck*). I continue to kiss your neck, once again nibbling at it and the groan comes once more. I move my right hand up to your left breast and begin to massage it. Your nipple is already erect and I can feel it through the material of your bra. *(Excellent she is getting more aroused it is working)*. **FUEL** I reach behind and unhook one of the catches on your bra as I continue to kiss across your shoulders and then move back to your mouth. I undo the second catch and your bra falls away as you shimmy the straps from your shoulders. I move my mouth onto your breast and let my tongue flick across your hardened nipple. You let out a gasp of delight.

(*Good I feel a surge inside*). **FUEL.** I continue moving my mouth about your breast, sucking and licking as you move your fingers around to the back of my head and pull my head tighter to you.

"Oh yes, that feels so good," you remark.

(*I feel the power rising now– excellent*) **FUEL.** I lift my mouth and speak.

"Like that do you?"

"Mmm yes, don't stop."

(*Good she loves this*). **FUEL.** I let my hands go under your skirt, pushing it up as I alternate between lightly scratching at your thighs and bottom and pressing my fingers against your toned flesh. You respond with more noises of pleasure.

(*All good so far – I can feel the power rising inside of me – this is going well – she cannot resist me*) **FUEL**

I push you onto the bed and you fall back into a sitting position. I push you back at the shoulder and you yield. I can see the excitement in your widening eyes as you fall backwards. (*See how she is looking at me, I can feel the power surging*) **FUEL**

"Take off your skirt," I order throatily. You nod (*Good she is doing what I want I am in control here she is submitting*). **FUEL.**

You remove the skirt and I return my mouth to your breasts as I begin to massage you through your panties. I can hear your breathing has become more ragged and you are pulling at me, trying to reach me through my trousers.

*(Yes, it is all working, she wants me, she wants me).* **FUEL.**

"Take your pants off," you urge. (*Oh yes she wants me.*)**FUEL.**

*(Time to exert some control here)*

"Not yet, plenty of time for that." You give a look of surprise but your mouth twists into a smile of delight. (*Yes, she likes me being in control – a little denial there worked a treat*) **FUEL.**

I slide down your panties and push your thighs apart as I begin to rub you in between your legs. You squirm in pleasure and we kiss again. (*All good – she is mine for sure I wonder how wet she is, let's find out*) **FUEL.**

I slip a finger inside of you and the warm, wetness is apparent. You sigh and I begin to stroke slowly your clit as you make more murmuring noises of delight. (*She loves this, I knew she would*) **FUEL.** I alternate my stroking motion between long slow strokes and then fast and urgent flicking. You are pressing upwards against my fingers as I allow one to slide inside you. You are wet and hot and our mouths are pressed against one another, tongues wrapped around one another. Your noises of appreciation are coming repeatedly as I allow a second finger to slide inside you and I start a beckoning motion, gently caressing the spongy area of your G spot. The effect causes a loud gasp to be emitted by you and you break off kissing me to look into my eyes with admiration and desire.

*(She is totally into this now. She is easily mine)* **FUEL.**

"God this is so good," you say, "I want you so much."

*(The power if really surging through me now, she is becoming ensnared, best say something in return.)* **FUEL.**

"I know, you are so beautiful and so delicious, I can't wait to be inside you."

"Oh fuck yes do it, fuck me now."

*(A little swearing, duly noted, she would like some filth whispered in her ears no doubt. She is mine to do, as I will.)* **FUEL.**

"Not yet my darling, I have to taste you." Your eyes widen in desire and I note you bite your lower lip. **FUEL.**

I begin kissing your thighs and you murmur some more as I make my way to your soaking slit. I kiss you lightly as I wriggle into a comfortable position at the foot of the bed. I lift my head and wait. *(I will stop for a moment and she will think there is something wrong, that she does not taste good and then when I continue she will love it even more when it is tinged with a dash of relief)* You notice I have stopped and you raise your head.

"What is it?" you ask a slightly nervous glance towards your nether regions.

"Nothing, just pass me a pillow please, I will be here for a while and I don't want to get a crick in my neck," I answer. You give a mock expression of outraged delight. **FUEL**

You oblige and reach behind you passing the pillow, which I slide under your bottom.

"I love your bottom, deliciously pert," I comment and you smile at my compliment. **FUEL**

I return to my task and engage my urgent mouth on you, licking and probing with my tongue, lightly nibbling with my lips, my tongue pushing inside you and then licking across your clit. You are moaning and grinding against me as I bury my face deep in you.

(*Make some appreciative noises as if you are eating a delicious ice cream, they always worry the first time you go down on them*) I make the noises of pleasure and you respond by thrusting harder against me. **FUEL**.

(*Keep this going for some time, most men do not do this for long enough, she will love the fact you have done this judging by the noise she is making, keep at it, she loves it.*)

I continue with my mouth and tongue feeling the power washing over me with every murmur and groan you make. The noises are becoming louder and more urgent.

"Oh god I am going to come," you announce.

(*Stop, make her want more, she will be intrigued and admire your discipline*)

I halt and move away.

"Don't stop, Jesus please don't stop," you urge. **FUEL.**

"Oh I am not stopping, I am just getting started."

I remove my trousers and underwear as you look on at my swollen cock. I pull on it ensuring it remains hard.

(*She is going to love this; I have her right where I want her. I am going to take her to heaven because only I can do that for her.*)

You look at me with almost animalistic desire. **FUEL.**

"Oh yes, take me now, I have wanted this from the moment I saw you." **FUEL.**

(*Oh, she wants me all right, better lay on some more sugar, she needs to know I feel the same, she wants the reassurance*).

"I was about to say the same thing. I want you so much. I don't think I have ever felt so turned on."

I crawl onto the bed as you move up it and I kiss you long and hard before I move in between your legs. I push the tip of my cock against you causing you to moan once again. **FUEL.**

"Yes do it, fuck me."

"Oh I am going to fuck you alright; I am going to fuck you until you scream." I respond as I push into you. You yield and groan as I begin to thrust inside of you. **FUEL**

I pay attention to each noise you make and when I hear your moans of delight, I repeat the movement, touch or caress. I alternate my rhythm as I embrace you and then lower my mouth to your breasts before moving back to your mouth again.

"I had to feel myself inside of you; you feel like silk, "I whisper.

"This is so good," you reply. **FUEL.**

*(Time to make her cum, put her before me, she will love that.)*

I break off from making love to you and I then kiss your neck, your breasts and then down over your stomach.

"Time for you to come," I growl.

"Oh yes, do it, please do it." **FUEL**

"I need to taste you again, you taste so sweet."

I return my mouth between your legs and with a combination of my fingers and my mouth; I bring you to a noisy climax. **FUEL.** I move back up to you as you lie there shuddering slightly and I wrap my arms around you.

"That was great," you smile with your eyes half-closed. **FUEL.**

"I just love hearing you moaning in that way and knowing I have caused it."

"Oh you cause it all right, that was terrific." **FUEL**

*(Lie next to her for a while and keep the compliments coming, she will keep throwing them back after that magnificent display.)*

"What about you?" you ask as your hand reaches for me.

"Oh I am fine, I am saving that for later, we are not finished yet, and you just turn me on so much."

You smile again. **FUEL.**

"Mmm I am up for that, you certainly know what you are doing," you say.

**FUEL.**

*(Of course, I do, I listen to every sound you make and watch you for movements, which signify what you like best in what I am doing. I am brilliant at making women climax. Always have been. I am brilliant at everything I do. I will start again on her in a moment and this time really fuck her hard and then I will hold her afterwards until she falls asleep. I do not need to be home anytime soon and I like it being here.)*

    I lie back holding you feeling the power surging through me after that superb performance which has left you satisfied (for now) and feeling close to me. The virtuoso performance will be the first of many tonight. I am not especially bothered in my own climax. It will be pleasant enough when it happens. I am far more interested in proving what an accomplished lover I am to you, making you want me even more and drinking deep of the fuel that you are pouring out for me. Do you see how my thoughts are pre-occupied with ensuring you feel good? I never reflect on how it feels physically for me. I enjoy the power I feel as the fuel is sucked up from you. That is what excites and enlivens me. I do not feel close to you, I do not feel affectionate or loving. Of course, I will show all these emotions and say the accompanying words because I know this is what you have come to expect. I will reflect back at you what you want and expect from our sexual union. I will say all the right things, hold you, stroke your hair afterwards and remark how nobody has made me feel this way before. I will flatter and compliment as my love bombing of you continues. It is not one-way however. I am getting plenty from you. I am getting the fuel I want, I am creating your addiction to me and I am setting you up to crave sexual liaison with me in readiness of me taking it away from you.

You will notice how my mind does not drift to other things or other people. I am entirely focussed on you because I want you to feel fantastic because of me bedding you for the reasons I have explained above. I am entirely geared towards your satisfaction and delight because then you give me what I need. I do not feel any warmth towards you because I find you physically attractive or an interesting person (although I acknowledge that you are both of those things) what draws me to you is your capacity for providing me fuel. That is all that matters to me. How much fuel will you give me? How often will you give it to me? How potent will it be? More fuel, often and of a high quality and the greater my interest in you. This will cause me to want to keep you. I will demonstrate more of the loving façade that you want (believing it to be real) in order to keep you supplying this fuel to me. There is no better way than demonstrating this loving façade than through the provision of delicious, orgasmic and satisfying sex.

That is what occupies my thoughts. How much fuel you will give me if I do this or that. Will you like me doing this to you or that to you? What should I say and do to create the 'moment' you want. How can I fulfil your expectations of a satisfying and enjoying sexual encounter? I will of course have laid the groundwork for this through finding out the things you like. I will have done this prior to us going to bed but once we have crossed that threshold and embarked on a sexual relationship I will demonstrate a high sexual appetite for you. This happens for several reasons. The first, as usual, is because the more I bed you the more fuel you will give me. The more times I take you to bed and deliver a wonderful performance (and it is like actors on a stage – it is not real) the closer you will bind to me. The more you will want me. The more you will want this when I later take it away from you. The more often I engage with you in sexual congress the more opportunities I have to find out what works (and what does not work) for you. Practice makes perfect.

I have no interest in feeling close to you. I have no interest in making you feel happy (other than the fuel that arises from it). I am robotic in my approach. I assess and observe and work out what I should be doing and saying to get the maximum reaction from you. I am considering the best way of getting fuel from you through sex. That is what I am thinking.

# The Types of Sexual Narcissist

In the same way that outside of the narcissistic sphere people have differing sexual appetites and differing sex drives, there are similar considerations to those of us within the narcissistic sphere. One cannot ignore sex. As I mentioned at the outset of this book it is everywhere and it influences everything. We may exist in our own created reality but sex resides there, in a greater of lesser extent, as well. Outside of this sphere, there are those who would be described as frigid. Within frigidity, one sees individuals who have no interest in sex whatsoever. They will not initiate it and they are not aroused when another tries to initiate sex with them. Some once had a sexual interest in their partner and it has gone but they remain amenable to sexual stimulation either with someone else or more typically alone. There again there are some people who once enjoyed sex with their partner but no longer do and they have no interest in sex at all, be it with someone else or with themselves. Also outside of this sphere, there are those who might be classed as demonstrating nymphomania (women) or satyriasis (men) whereby they have a particularly heightened urge to engage in sexual activity. I understand the term hyper sexuality is now used as a catch-all for this behaviour. Then in between these two extremes come those who have sex often but would not be described as having an overriding urge to engage in sexual activity, those who engage in periodically with their current partner, others who occasionally have an extra-marital fumble, those who rarely engage in sexual activity but when they do they certainly enjoy it. The desire for sexual activity and its frequency is a vast scale. You will find our kind at various points along this scale as well. Similarly the sexual appetite of people is fascinating and varied. This ranges from those activities enjoyed by the majority (for example mutual masturbation, oral sex and penetrative sex) through to more niche areas involving BDSM, role-play, group sex and on to other areas which the moral majority may regard as dark, depraved, weird or just wrong. It is a broad church again and it is one which is certainly visited by our kind. As a consequence of my own personal sexual experiences and the observation and considered study of others of my kind that I know, I have determined four classes of sexual narcissist. Each class will engage in sex to some degree and will engage in different types of sexual activity in varying extents but they approach, use and regard sex in different ways.

## The Victim Variety

The Victim Variety of sexual narcissist is somebody who lacks the body and looks obsession of the somatic narcissist and also lacks the intellect of the cerebral narcissist. He is typically a low-functioning narcissist since he does not inherently have the wit or intelligence to seduce his victims through words and demonstrations of intellectual brilliance. Neither does he have the drive or discipline to take care of himself physically, dress well, and have a rigorous hygiene and looks maintenance ritual. He is however a narcissist and need to seduce his victims all the same and he do so by presenting as a victim who needs looking after.

I cannot speak personally for those members of our club who are frankly letting the side down but I am aware of them having witnessed them in action. I tend to think that these narcissists are not particularly high functioning and they do not tune themselves in to their victim sexually the way they ought to in the way that someone like me will. They also do not tend to love-bomb hugely effectively but instead they merely hide their savage side in the initial stages so they are at least not off-putting. I also tend to think that they draw their victims in not by a show of supremacy and strength but rather by eliciting sympathy. They play on the empath's sense of caring and nurturing and present as a victim in order to be mothered by the empath. Accordingly, they do not exhibit the same degree of allure, charisma and all around sparkling brilliance as we do. They are still able to draw people in because there are caregivers who do not care so much about how someone looks and so on, but feel sorry for them and wants to care for them and make them better. Similarly, they exhibit no brilliance between the sheets and may even demonstrate incompetence in order to draw further sympathy and invite the caring empath to teach them to be better. These narcissists are entirely self-centred and lack the charm and tools to draw their victims in with brilliance and magnificence. These narcissists do tend to be from the lower functioning variety that is not especially good at anything. They will provide some embellishment but again because they are low- functioning they will lack the intelligence, guile and wit to conjure up fantastic tales of achievement and accomplishment. Instead, they need to keep their abusive streak in check, something they are able to do but they need to find some other way of drawing in their victims. They cannot hold up anything shiny or sparkling in the way that most of our kind does. Instead, they do the reverse. What they exhibit is rusting, battered and dented but they do it in a "Shucks look at me, I am in a bit of a mess, and I need someone to help me out, would that kind person be you?" They present their victim status very early on and this will not be attractive to many people but it will draw certain people to them, those who want to care for them, mother them and make them become better. They will see the narcissist as a bit of a rough diamond which needs polishing up and they are just the person to do this.

Since this type of narcissist does not rely on being a shining beacon of attraction to people but rather a battered old vehicle which needs some tender loving care he sees no reason to let the flattery flow. There is little in the way of grandiose gestures or extravagance. Instead he will just play the victim card repeatedly in order to keep that empath looking after him and drawn to him. He is appreciative of the attention and caring and why not? He is gaining fuel but is also being looked after. He will probably not work and rely on the financial ability of the victim in that respect. He will help a little, just enough to avoid reprimand and enough to draw thanks from the empath. He keeps the abuse in check and therefore whilst never over the top in word or gesture he is pleasant enough. He certainly is not horrible His gratitude at being looked after and given attention by the empath satisfies the empath and they are willing to overlook the deficiencies because they feel good about taking care of this person. Since this type of narcissist has no need to look good, sound great and shine this attitude pervades into the sexual arena. He need not make his partner feel orgasmic and on a higher place. She will just be grateful he made the effort. In that way that all empaths make excuses she will regard his ineptitude between the sheets as just another item that makes him seem lovable and charming. Okay, he is not the world's best lover, he is not even in the top thousand but he tries and that is all the empath in such a relationship, as this will want. The empath may just be happy to have someone to share his or her life with and care for. The empath may not be overly bothered about sex themselves and therefore this type of low functioning narcissist finds a home readily enough. Some of you may recognise an individual like this. For them, sex is not a weapon because they have no need of it. It does not fit with their make-up. They are not scintillating like me and others like me and therefore being a sexual superstar is unnecessary. As I have mentioned in other writings, we are not only creatures of economy but we have been created economically. We do not like to expend energy unnecessarily. It is also the case that if it is not going to gather us fuel we do not need it. In the way that we are not furnished with empathy or the capacity for the remorse, because they do not gather any fuel for us, the low functioning narcissist is not blessed with sexual prowess, as it serves no purpose for him. He will only seek out those that want to mother him. He will not seek out those who want to be taken to sexual nirvana repeatedly. He will not need to use this sexual weapon to charm his victim because his helplessness and victim status does that for him instead. Accordingly, many of these low functioning narcissists either have little interest in sex or are useless at it.

Sex is still a material factor in the relationship with the Victim Variety because he will exhibit incompetence in this arena so that the caring empath feels sorry for him and will even feel a need to try and teach him. Some narcissists who are of the Victim Variety will go even further and demonstrate varying degrees of frigidity, which I touched on at the beginning of this chapter. Once again, this is designed to draw out sympathy from the empath. It is also done to garner sexual attention as well. By exhibiting no interest or little interest in sex or even appearing impotent, the desire to fix will be overwhelming for the empath who will do her best to try to light the fire of desire in this low-functioning narcissist. As it has been said

"To succeed with the opposite sex, tell her you're impotent. She can't wait to disprove it."

This will result in the empath providing plenty of fuel to this type of sexual narcissist in order to try to make him better or 'cure' him.

## The Cerebral Narcissist

The Cerebral Narcissist has a limited interest in sex, certainly of the physical variety. This type of narcissist prefers to flaunt his brilliant intellect as the method by which he seduces his victims. He has little interest in engaging in actual sexual relations because that is not his forte. His magnificence stems from his high intellect, his amazing memory and his capacity for complexity. It is the repeated tales of academic achievement, cerebral power and scintillating intellect, which are used to wow and overpower the resistance. The cerebral narcissist is well read, extensively schooled and excels in showering all who will listen with evidence of his intellectual superiority. Such brilliance proves highly attractive to a certain section of empathic individuals who wish to engage a brain that is the size of a planet. The conversations, albeit one-sided, are nevertheless stimulating and engrossing. There is never a silence for the cerebral narcissist is always primed to provide you with an interesting fact about the champagne that you are both drinking and a historical anecdote concerning the Ponte Vecchio that you are walking over. This walking almanac of facts and opinions is quite dazzling and vastly appealing to some.

In terms of how sex fits into this equation, there are chiefly two points to note. The cerebral narcissist will engage in sex periodically if the intellectual avenue becomes exhausted. The sex will not be fulfilling for either party owing to the fact that the cerebral narcissist is neither interested in this nor particularly proficient. It will be done when the intellectual charm is not working as well as it once did and is often done out of a sense of obligation. The cerebral narcissist will feel that every so often he is obligated to discharge his marital responsibilities by engaging in sex with his partner. This is purely done in order to maintain the happiness of the other individual during the golden period and during devaluation, the cerebral narcissist will effectively become frigid, as he will have no interest or sense of obligation to engage in sexual relations with his victim.

The cerebral narcissist however will often talk about sex during the seduction stage. Words are very much the weapons of the narcissist and especially so with the higher functioning of our kin. The cerebral narcissist although uninterested in the physical side of sex, will still wish to show off his vast knowledge of the subject. He will want to regale you with his knowledge of sexual literature, sexual analysis and sexual awareness. He will have read many books about the subject. That is not to enable him to be a better lover but to allow him to be a better speaker about being a lover. The cerebral narcissist will engage in seductive letter writing, often of the old school romantic variety. He will tease and titillate using text messages and telephone messages. He will quite readily, purely for the purpose of seduction, talk dirty down the telephone to you whilst you masturbate. He may tell you he is doing the same but he will not as the physical sensation is of no interest to him. What arouses him is the intellectual power he has in being able to use his lexicon of love to arouse you down the telephone line. Your noises of appreciation and compliments provide him with the fuel he requires, he demonstrates how knowledgeable he is about sex by talking in this manner and he has the added bonus of not having to engage in the actual act. This suits the cerebral narcissist most well. There will be plenty of opportunities for him to exhibit his wide knowledge of sexual practices in order to heighten your anticipation and to wow you as you listen wide-eyed to his explanations of certain techniques and behaviours and what they achieve. He knows all about sex but he certainly does not put it into practice. That is beneath him. In the way that those with a suntan were once looked down upon because this denoted being a manual labourer, the cerebral narcissist looks down on the actual sexual act as beneath him. Why engage in something so crass, something so animalistic and frankly barbaric (other than out of a sense of occasional duty to maintain the façade of the golden period) when one can use the pristine cleanliness of a beautiful mind to gain that all-important fuel? I have a cousin who is a little younger than I am. He is the offspring of my Uncle Peter (who you can read all about in **Fury**) and has been created in the same way as Uncle Peter but he does not have the interest in sex preferring to use his excellent academic credentials and brilliant mind to effect his acquisition of fuel. My cousin finds the act of sexual intercourse so abhorrent because he sees it as beneath someone with such a fine mind as him that on the few occasions he has been compelled to do it, he runs off to the bathroom afterwards and vomits. Not only does he not like the intimacy that comes with the act of coitus but the noise, the fluids, the interaction of parts from which one urinates all disgusts him as he has told me, to my amusement, on many occasions.

Accordingly, should you find that your narcissist is of the cerebral variety do not expect sexual fireworks. There will plenty of talk about that and he will arouse your with words but there will be little delivery between the sheets.

## The Somatic Narcissist

Here comes the gym bunny that has a bottom so tight it will bounce off the walls before he bounces you all around the bedroom. The Somatic Narcissist is obsessed with his or her physical appearance. They diet fastidiously, put the hours in at the gym, select the clothing which allows them to flaunt their bodies and spend a lot of time with their favourite person; their reflection in the mirror. They look for reactions of admiration to their beauty, their physical perfection, their muscular appearance and smart and attractive appearances. The Somatic Narcissist likes to demonstrate athletic ability by showing his body can throw the furthest, run the fastest or dive the deepest. The appearance of his or her body and what can be achieved through it (strength, flexibility, and endurance) are what matter in order to draw fuel from their victims.

This fixation with the body means that the arena of sex is hugely important to the Somatic Narcissist. He wants to look terrific whilst having sex so you coo and purr over that finely honed body, the impressive biceps and rigid six-pack. Not only that but look at how he can have sex for a long time as he flips you from this position to the next like a piece of meat. His stamina is legendary, his ability to get you and him into all manner of positions should be respected and admired and all of this is achieved whilst looking like a Greek god. Whereas the cerebral narcissist uses his intellect to conquer, the somatic narcissist uses his or her body to achieve the same outcome. His body is designed for admiration and where better to achieve that than in the bedroom.

The Somatic Narcissist will also demonstrate the legendary hypocrisy for which we are known. You must not compete with him in any way in the looks department but you are expected to look your best because you are an extension of him. You must not gain weight, have bad skin, wear ill-fitting clothes or forget to shave your legs. You must walk the tightrope of ensuring that you fit in with his image of bodily perfection whilst at the same time not pulling the spotlight away from him. The Somatic Narcissist will excel during the seductive stage because the twin allure of somebody looking so good and performing so brilliantly between the sheets will blow you away. You will receive premium quality sex, amazing orgasms, grade A sexual encounters. His stamina is vast, his eagerness and readiness to copulate is staggering and you will be the beneficiary in all of this. This is just a fortunate coincidence for you because as with all types of our kind, the Somatic Narcissist is just after your fuel. You may not regard this as such a problem during the seduction phase. So what if he gets off on your screams of pleasure and your repeated appreciation of those defined forearms and pectoral muscles, you are being given the sexual time of your life, he deserves the praise doesn't he? Naturally, this is how we want it to work. You give us the fuel, have no realisation what you are doing, and therefore have no concern, so consequently you embrace it wholeheartedly. When the devaluation occurs, you can expect the somatic narcissist to maintain still a rampant sexual appetite but the last thing on his mind will be making you purr with pleasure. You will be taken against your will, subjected to lengthy sexual hammerings as he focusses on how brilliant he is at lasting so long, how glorious his taut muscles look as he ploughs away at you. There is no consideration for whether you are enjoying yourself or even if you are being physically hurt because all that matters to him is how good he looks and how masterful he is in the sack. If you were to vanish from beneath him, he would barely notice. The somatic narcissist is in effect having sex with himself. He is so fine to look at that he would eat himself if he could and similarly he would engage in sexual intercourse with himself if that were a possibility. Masturbation ranks high with narcissists anyway for the reasons I have pointed out earlier but this action is even more prevalent with the somatic narcissist. He will position himself in front a mirror and as he plays with himself, he will admire how he looks and this reinforces his need for you to admire him also. The somatic narcissist will bombard you with pictures of his buff body and his penis during the seduction stage. He will also do this with online strangers in order to gain their admiration also.

Exhibiting their physicality is necessary for the somatic variety of our kind. Accordingly, you can expect sexual gymnastics during the seduction phase and then to be slapped, smacked, bent over, throttled, pinned down and all other manifestations of physical dominance. The fear in your eyes as he pins you to the bed and takes what he regards as his only goes to fuel him further. Any kind of treatment, which emphasises his physical prowess and superiority, will be meted out in the sexual arena and invariably you will suffer consequently. You can expect to be humiliated, dominated and shoved around by the somatic narcissist during devaluation. You are little more than a blow-up doll to him, which is to be manipulated into all manner of positions all in order to make him look magnificent. You are expected to be grateful for the sexual pounding you have received and if your praise is not forthcoming then expect consequences as this inherent criticism will ignite his rage. Rather than rely on withering put downs and caustic comments, the somatic narcissist will lash out physically, again underpinning his physical superiority whilst storing away your transgression for use in the sexual arena at a later date. The somatic narcissist will insist on bondage, your subjugation being a natural consequence of his superiority. You will be bent over his knee and smacked with his hand or a cane. I know of one narcissist who would apply nettles to his scrotum because he explained it gave him a massive and sustained erection, notwithstanding the pain and he expected his victim to endure the application of those nettles to her nipples, bottom and thighs in order to heighten her sexual experience also. In the hands of the somatic narcissist, sex is a highly charged weapon. It is with the somatic narcissist that you will experience the greatest highs during the sexual seduction and the humiliating and hurtful lows when the devaluation occurs. Much of what is written below is the preserve of the somatic narcissist.

## The Elite Narcissist

Sex plays a part in all of the categories of sexual narcissist. The Victim Variety uses it to engender sympathy and attention be it a lack of interest and/or incompetence in sex. The cerebral narcissist talks a great sexual game but has little interest in its practical application save the occasional bout of sex out of obligation. The somatic narcissist is a sexual dynamo who is at his fore in the sexual arena, forsaking cleverness and intellect for the dominance of muscle and looks. The final category of sexual narcissist is the Elite Narcissist. He combines both the looks and physical supremacy of the somatic narcissist with the intellect and spoken charm of the cerebral narcissist. The Elite Narcissist will talk you into bed and deliver as well. He will have your mind aroused and then your body. He may not be quite the sexual champion that the somatic narcissist is but he is no slouch. He will look after himself and be trim and athletic if not ripped and buff, but such a look is not beyond him. He may not have the cranial magnificence of the cerebral narcissist but again he is no dribbling idiot. He has plenty of intelligence and wit, which he puts to good use. This combination of intelligence and looks creates the deadliest narcissist because he can use to both charm and seduce you and then use both to devalue you. Hence, he is categorised as an elite member of our club.

The Elite Narcissist is interested in sex because he recognises that sex comes in many forms. He knows that is can be the sensual whisper in your ear or the raunchy text messaging he sends you. He knows it is the athletic and sudden performance in a penthouse suit and the gentle, tender lovemaking that you crave. He has none of the disgust for the sexual act like the cerebral narcissist and does not rely solely on physical domination like the somatic narcissist. He is able to combine both worlds and straddle the same in order to exact his manipulations. Where the mouth leads, his body will follow and you are subjected to the one-two combination. Whilst the Victim Variety needs the mothering empath, the Cerebral Narcissist needs the disciple empath who worships at this temple of knowledge, the Somatic Narcissist needs the empath who is swayed by looks, and the Elite Narcissist just needs somebody with empathic qualities. They may not be a complete empath but the everyday charm and attractiveness of the Elite Narcissist will seduce someone who may have lower empathic qualities than normal. Naturally, the Elite Narcissist will be using sex (in word and deed) to ensnare an empath, a super-empath or a co-dependent but he is able to mine fuel from some of the lesser prospects. The Elite Narcissist will use the spoken charm and knowledge of the Cerebral Narcissist and meld it with the sexual physical allure of the Somatic Narcissist to create a very potent sexual magnet indeed. Few can resist him and the sex he grants is gratifying on many levels. For the same reason, when the Elite Narcissist commences the devaluation, his victim his subjected to a further double whammy as spoken word and physical act are used against her. The effect is devastating.

You will recognise the type of the narcissist you have been entangled with or perhaps you still are, from these four categories. As you read on, keep in mind their key characteristics as I discuss other elements of sex and the narcissist.

# Why Are We So Good At Sex?

I am a sexual Olympian. I know I am. I am always good at what I do. I deliver and sex is not different. I have never had any complaint about my sexual performance (at least in the seduction stage) from anyone I have coupled with. Whether they have been someone I have engaged in a relationship with, a casual and repeated friend with benefits or a one-night stand, I have always been praised for my sexual technique. I have to be praised because that gives me fuel. In order to get this praise I need to be brilliant. You think I am really into you if I can deliver such an orgasmic experience. I am not into you. I am into the fuel you give me from your reaction to my technique.

Speaking in general terms my kind and I are brilliant between the sheets. More than anything else, after the devaluation has begun and the eventual discard comes about, I hear comments such as these.

"He was the best I have ever had"

"He was a bastard but boy did he know how to make me come."

"He would shout at me and I would shout back and then he would have me. I hated him but at the same time loved how he did that to me."

"He knew exactly what to do to turn me on and he knew exactly what to do turn me off. He was a sexual mind reader."

"Of all the things I miss, I miss sleeping with him the most."

"I know he will love it when I say this but he was the best lover that I have ever had."

I know it is not just me about whom this is said. I know from the encounters that other people have they usually praise the sexual performance of the narcissist they became entangled with and they miss it afterwards. Before I engage in explaining why most of our kind are fantastic at sex, let me address the issue of the under and non-performers in our ranks.

Most narcissists are sexual dynamos. High sexual appetites, broadminded, attentive and accomplished lovers. Now, I appreciate that this is not always the case. I know that some of our kind have very little interest in sex and there are those of our number who have sexual dysfunction and are not anything special at all between the sheets. I have referred above to the sexual appetites and outlooks of the Victim Variety and the Cerebral Narcissist who are not proficient in the physical side of sexual activity. We are not concerned with understanding why they are so good at sex because they are not.

As I described above, the true sexual conquerors are the somatic and the elite varieties of narcissist who are sexually proficient and use sex very much as a weapon in order to further their aims.

I belong to the elite. The elite narcissist uses both intelligence and sex to snare his victims. Being of a higher functioning capability, we of the elite variety use our intelligence to ensure we are sexual warriors.

Imagination, perception, guile, charm is all in large supply and when sprayed liberally around in the sexual arena they heighten and improve our sexual performances.

Thus, if you are coupled with a narcissist who has little interest in sex or is not very good at it they are either a low functioning victim type or a high functioning cerebral narcissist. Either way, sex is not a weapon for them. They rely on victimhood or intellect instead.

If you are lucky enough to be paired with a somatic narcissist who is body and sex obsessed or an elite narcissist who combines high function with sexual recognition then you will have a fantastic time between the sheets. Somatic and elite narcissists use sex as their weapons. Accordingly, that weapon needs to be effective, reliable and devastating. Soldiers are effective because they come well equipped, well trained and they know how to use their skills and equipment. We are just the same. We come equipped with many sexual skills, we know how to use them and we are well practised. This leads to us to examine why it is we are so good at sex.

We have many sexual partners. As with anything in life, the more you do something, the better you become at it. If you play football infrequently, you will not be particularly good. You may have some innate talent but that needs to be flexed and honed. If you play regularly, your skill set will improve. If you play the same team week in week out then you will improve but only so far. If you play many teams on many different occasions, you will learn more and become a lot better. The same applies to us. We have many sexual partners so this enables us to become better lovers with skills that are more practised and a greater awareness of what people enjoy and do not enjoy. Happily, for us we derive several benefits from these partners. Firstly, they are differing suppliers of fuel. Secondly, we can use them to draw fuel from others by triangulating. Thirdly, they help us hone our sexual ability.

We are masters of observation. We need to observe the way other people behave to further our own ambitions. There are several reasons why we must watch others:-

1. To mimic behaviours because we have not generated certain feelings and behaviours ourselves;

2. To understand what people like and do not like so we can mirror that behaviour and reflect it back at them;

3. To gather fuel since this is all about your reactions to us. We must be observing to receive the reaction;

Accordingly, we not only spend many time observing people but we also ensure we remember all of the detail we accumulate in performing this action. This skill at observation provides a particular dividend when applied to sexual relations. We are experts at noticing what works for you. We are alerted to your reactions not only by what you say, but by the tone of your words, the sound of your breathing, the flush on your chest and cheeks, the expression on your face, the pout of your mouth, the way your knees are pointing, the fact your wrists are being shown to us, the way you take a drink, the widening of your eyes and so on. We notice all these cues and in an instant, we know whether something is working or not. If it is not we have such a vast sexual repertoire (because remember we have been exposed to many different sexual partners who all have different ways in being pleasured but also have also been willing to impart their knowledge to us) we can they reach for a different method and apply it. We are never stuck for ideas as to how to please you in bed. Ally this with our lack of boundary recognition and we are likely to try anything. Add on top of this our boundless self-confidence and sense of entitlement to be a wonderful lover, then we are one. Ask any sportsman what is the key ingredient in being successful and he will answer that it is confidence. A confident golfer will try the difficult drives and the audacious thirty-foot putt. A confident striker will bang the goals in for fun without hesitation or concern. If you think you are good at something, you will be good at something. We are the same. We know we are brilliant and so it comes to be. Whatever we turn our hands to, we do well and sex is no different.

We are also masters of creating illusions. We create the perfect environment for you to have the optimum sexual experience. I do not just mean all the ways we might touch and caress you, but the environment we create for it all to take place. We know for example that you have always wanted to be made love to in a room overlooking Rome in the summer so we give this to you. We know you want to dance in a beautiful hotel before being whisked up a sweeping staircase to a four-poster bed. We know you want to watch romantic film in one another's arms before we slowly kiss and undress you. We are wizards at the seductive sentence and charming compliment and we will shower you with these to heighten your experience. With us colours seems brighter, sounds are more melodious and your senses are magnified. We do not just make love to you in a wonderful way. We do it in a beautiful place, on a special occasion, with everything better. We give you the entire package and in doing so, we are exacerbating the fraud. By creating this perfect environment, you are being conditioned to expect the experience to be even better. Who can fail to be taken to an orgasmic heaven when presented with such a beautifully arrange and constructed environment? We are maximising our chances of pleasing you by setting the stage. It is akin to a film set. We control the lighting, the soundtrack, the make-up, the props, the script and the positioning of everything as we manufacture this glorious environment. Once established we put you into the middle of it all and then unleash our arsenal of sexual experience and brilliance. The result is that you have no chance. Not only are we excellent when we have sex with you, we make it seem even better than it actually is because we set the scene appropriately.

To enable us to do this we must understand what it is that you want and expect. I have written above about how you are conditioned to believe that love and sex occur in a certain way. We buy into that and harness it to ensure that it is provided to you for your delight. You believe what authors and scriptwriters, advertising agencies and agony aunts churn out so who are we to deny that to you? We do not. We recognise what you want and what you expect and we give it to you. We are attuned to what you desire, both consciously and subconsciously and in giving you the very thing you want we can only succeed. The converse of this applies also. We know what you do not like, what troubles and concerns you so we are able to avoid making those errors and falling into a trap. Of course, we will use this knowledge for our nefarious purposes at a later stage when we begin our devaluation of you but that comes in a later chapter. For now, our ability to understand what you like enables us to deliver for you time and time again.

Ultimately, our sexual prowess is driven by our hunger for fuel. We know that you will give us more fuel and of a potent variety if we send you to heaven between the sheets. There is no greater incentive to us than knowing we are going to be doused in sweet, potent fuel by you. This encourages us to expend our energies in your favour. We would not allow this to happen without the guarantee of there being fuel at the end. The prospect of wallowing in your love, admiration and adoration as you lie there panting, praising us and sending us those looks and speaking those words of total admiration spurs us on considerably.

Knowing that we will be drawing fuel from you encourages us to perform to the highest standard. It is akin to an employee being motivated because of securing a significant financial bonus. In our case, the stakes are higher. If we not get this fuel it will affect our very existence and therefore it is paramount we acquire it. We have done our preparatory work to target someone who will provide us with fuel and is someone who is susceptible to our overtures. We need this fuel to be delivered soon and that is why we go hell for leather in our seduction. This is why we want to get you into bed as soon as we can. It is not because we are desperate for the physical sensation of sex. It is because we are desperate to sow the seeds of addiction and to enable us to start drawing fuel from you as quickly as possible. To enable us to do this we need to provide you with an unforgettable sexual experience. To achieve this we must know what turns you on, heighten the environment and deliver the desired product to you. Once you have experienced it the once you will want it again. We will make it appear that we are completely into you, that you turn us on, that you are so sexually compatible with us and we have never experienced anything like this. These are all lies. We are just telling you what you would like to her so that you feel a greater bond towards us. We are filling your ears with our sweet sedition in order to compel you to experience a heightened experience and in turn see us a solely responsible for your euphoria. We tell you that only you make us feel this way in order to dupe you into thinking the very same thing. We repeatedly tell you how we are linked on a sexual level so you will believe the same thing. We mirror what you want in order to tell you what we want you to feel for us. By tapping into your vast empathic reservoir, we are accessing a pool of fuel. You are a walking tanker of emotions. You act emotionally, you are governed by your emotions and you show them. That is why we want you. Sex is the most visceral and direct way of hooking up to you and pumping all that delicious fuel out of you. Brilliant sex equals brilliant fuel.

Accordingly, our sexual mastery arises from the following:-

- Repeated practice

- Varied sexual experiences with different partners

- Lack of inhibitions though no boundary recognition

- Self-belief

- Keen observation of responses and ability to adjust technique

- Driven by the reward of fuel

- Reflection. Giving you what you want.

A combination of all of the above results in us being brilliant at sex. Nevertheless, of course, we are only brilliant at it with you aren't we?

# The Sexual Identity

I mentioned above the different classes of narcissist that exist in the sexual sphere. It is also necessary to consider the concept of the sexual identity of the narcissist as this is a fluid and interesting area. You may be familiar with the fact that our kind creates and maintains a construct. This construct might be referred to as a cloak, a mask, or a shield. I provide more detail on this construct in **Fuel** and also in **Fury**. This construct imprisons the creature, which we must not allow to be freed for if we do it will spell the end for us. The construct is also the means by which we attract our victims. We are like magpies. If we see something shiny and attractive in someone else, we will take that fragment of their personality or life and attach it to our construct to make it our own and in turn make ourselves more attractive to the world. This means that we have little concept of ourselves because we become the very thing we consider as desirable to you in order to attract you to us. We take a fragment from one person, a section from another and a shard from yet another person, piecing them together to build our cloak. This many-pieced device is glittering, shining and scintillating and is so effective at attracting people. We allow this to define who and what we are for the purposes of seducing people into our world and so they then provide us with the fuel that we require so much.

This hijacking of the traits and identities of others allows us to portray ourselves as brilliant executives, highbrow scientists, and capable sportsmen, talented artists, possessing marvellous comedic timing, charming, interesting, attractive, beautiful, alluring, stimulating and desirable. The list of traits, which people find attractive is long and we will look to acquire as many of these as possible to add to our construct. By reflecting these traits towards our target, they become so much easier to ensnare as they are bedazzled by our magnificence. Imagine each trait is represented by a precious stone and soon you will see us possessing a peacock's tail of shimmering diamonds, emeralds, sapphires and rubies. Sparkling, glinting, and causing anyone who looks upon us to stare open-mouthed in awe and admiration.

Our behaviour is no different when it comes to the issue of sex. In the same way that we create our day-to-identity by purloining from others, we do the same with sexual identities. We will take a piece from other people's sexual preferences and identities in order to make ourselves more appealing to our target. If we establish, through our preparatory work, that you have a preference for bondage in a submissive role then we too will be happy to engage in bondage. If we learn that, you enjoy having food eaten from you, as you lie naked on a table we will explain how that is one of our favourite fetishes as well. It does not matter whether we find it appealing or not, that is irrelevant. We do not consider whether the act is something that people would regard as normal or morally outrageous. It is not something whereby we consider whether a particular preference is lurking at the darker end of the sexual spectrum. What interests us is that if we perform this particular act will it give us fuel? During the seduction stage, we will select those things, which you actively delight in and enjoy so that when we do this with you, you will offer up the sweet, positive fuel. When our devaluation of you takes place we are not concerned whether you like omorashi (the act of finding your own or someone else's urgent need to urinate arousing) but the fuel we derive from making you drink lots of water and sit still as you need the toilet, your facial expressions and protestations, is what we are interested in. We regard all of these as means to an end and of course, you will understand by now that with our kind the end always justifies the means. We have no opinion about whether the activity we engage in with you is deemed as perverse, abnormal or generally acceptable, all that matters is the fuel that comes with it. If you want to be smeared in birthday cake as we sing to you before spanking you because this turns you on and make you admire us for doing it, we will do it. Whatever you want we will do during the seduction stage because we will just mirror your desires.

This means that some narcissists will adopt any sexual preference in order to gather fuel. Homosexuality is a trait, which the narcissist will adopt. If the target is of the same sex and the use of a sexual liaison will deliver fuel to the narcissist then homosexual activity will be engaged in. Not all of our kind will operate this way. This may be as a consequence of the particular environment we find ourselves. If it is predominantly a heterosexual one, then sex will be used through this heterosexual conduit. I have no interest in homosexual encounters because I operate in an especially female environment. I also acknowledge that my preference for women stems from my upbringing, which is a topic for another occasion but worth mentioning in passing. I have no dislike for homosexuality and I would not rule it out if fuel was involved but I have never had cause to engage in such acts. Those narcissists who engage in homosexual activity are often, though of course not exclusively of a somatic nature. This is because they have such a high regard for their own physical form that seeing themselves replicated in another man proves highly attractive to them. The opportunity to in effect have sex with himself or herself proves irresistible to the narcissist and the fuel that flows from this appreciative partner is of a high quality. The narcissist will adopt the traits of others for the purposes of sexuality and also become interested in that other person if fuel is to be gathered. Sex, as a powerful tool that is available to primarily somatic and elite narcissists to gather this fuel will be used. This means that a narcissist will demonstrate bi-sexuality, interest in transvestitism and transgender individuals. These interests will yield fuel from the other person. Accordingly, the narcissist will develop a taste for lady boys because they provide fuel. They will cross-dress in order to prove attractive to someone who wants to provide fuel in that situation. It is also done in order to triangulate and draw additional fuel. The narcissist will delight, when devaluing a partner in trying to shock that person and they may do so by hinting at our revealing indulging in behaviours, which that partner may regard as 'deviant'. Their shocked reaction on finding their husband parading around the house in her panties and bra with a wig on will provide the narcissist with fuel. Put bluntly, a narcissist will more often than not engage in sexual behaviours with anyone in order to gather fuel. If this means being gay for the duration of the fuel gathering, then so be it. If this requires acting in a frigid manner to frustrate the partner and gather fuel, it will happen. Should it prove necessary to lie on a table and be milked through a glory hole to the appreciative murmurs of the lady under the table then the narcissist will do so.

Many people are shocked when they learn of their narcissist partner's predilection for engagement in so-called deviant behaviours. To the narcissist they are all on the same continuum. The act itself does not provide any greater or lesser sexual stimulation compared to other acts but what it might do is yield greater fuel. This is why narcissists will adopt the sexual identity of someone who engages in the more extreme elements of the sexual spectrum. It is not because the narcissist finds being dressed in a nappy and engaging in infantilism sexually arousing it is because the fuel on offer becomes greater than hand relief from a long-standing girlfriend. It is the fuel not the act that matters. It is the reaction of the participant and/or observer, which the narcissist wants, and they will engage in many seemingly bizarre activities to achieve this. With this knowledge when you next find your narcissist partner wearing a horse mask and masturbating in front of a webcam with a man wearing a similar horse mask in Santiago you may be shocked initially but the reality is it is the fuel that is the concern, not the wearing of the horse mask. If you find you have little choice but to remain with the narcissist you may eventually realise that these behaviours although bizarre are ultimately only about fuel. Of course, there are those amongst our kind who may venture into certain activities, which are illegal. This arises out of their failure to recognise boundaries, sense of entitlement and their ongoing quest to use sex to draw fuel. Those of our kind who do this have no fear of consequences, which may arise from those illegal acts as the fuel gained supersedes those concerns. Furthermore, those of our kind regard laws and conventions as inapplicable to us by reason of our superiority and they will not regard themselves as having done anything wrong. For myself I do not go down that route because I have too much I could lose and that successful edifice that I have created and which gathers me so much fuel would be lost. I cannot have that happen. I do not want the very thing I have created which garners so much fuel for me to be destroyed but then as a member of the elite, I am blessed with the higher function to recognise this and plan accordingly. Whilst I often leave chaos in my wake I am mindful to ensure that my fuel platform is not damaged and remains operating at all times. Those of our somatic brothers who may not be blessed with such higher cognitive functions are not as astute and it is amongst them you will find the paedophiles, rapists and such like. They of course will not regard that behaviour as something that is wrong for the reasons details above. They also will not have as great a regard for the edifice they have created and therefore are more likely to risk its destruction through detection, conviction and imprisonment. That is why the somatic members of our club are often the ones who foolishly engage in vicious assaults on their victims. That leaves evidence and being placed in segregation in a prison is a very hard place to obtain fuel. I hold the authorities in contempt but I am not so stupid as to ever give them a chance to take away my fuel and imprison me. I cannot say the same for others of our kind. However, all of that is a subject for discussion on another occasion.

The fact remains that the sexual identity of the narcissist is both ambiguous and fluid. If it moves and provides fuel, they will hump it. They will take on the traits and likes of the person they wish to engage with in a sexual union all for the purpose of obtaining fuel. The sexual activity is never vanilla and will range from the slightly unusual to the very bizarre but all of this will be initiated by the target. If the target enjoys having, an enema administered and then pressure applied to their stomach because it arouses them, the narcissist will willingly engage in this behaviour during the seduction stage in order to gather that fuel. Whatever the target wants in the seduction stage will be provided by the narcissist. If the target is gay, the narcissist will be gay. If the target likes to dress as a girl and be treated like a sissy, then the narcissist will play along as a dominant schoolteacher. So long as fuel is provided, the narcissist will oblige. This identify will also warp and shift for the purpose of gathering fuel in the devaluing process. The narcissist will engage in acts you find alarming or hurtful in order to draw fuel. The sadistic element of our kind will push their victim further and further in order to gain fuel, their mental and physical discomfort being of no concern and indeed an imperative in order for the sadistic narcissist to gain fuel from sexual humiliation, degradation and perversion. In terms of sexual identity, the narcissist is an amalgam of everybody else. They have no preferences since for the most part, they will engage in everything. By one turn, the sexual identity of the narcissist is complex and elusive and then by another it is obvious and ubiquitous. Understanding this attitude of the narcissist to adopting the sexual traits and preferences of others is key to realising why the narcissist behaves in the sexual arena as he or she does. As ever, at the heart of this chameleon like behaviour is the need for fuel.

# The Seduction Stage

The seduction stage is the opening act of our entanglement with you. This is where we come at you with our campaign of love bombing. The nasty and abusive sides to our characters will be hidden well away beneath a mask of charm. We bombard you with love and charm in order to sweep you off your feet. It is a tsunami of seduction and it is designed to cause you to ignore warning sides, fall desperately in love with, bond closely to us and ultimately provide us with fuel. We deploy an array of manipulative techniques when we undertake this love bombing. All of these techniques are pleasant and desirable. They often seem over the top but the warning that comes with that is usually ignored because nearly everybody likes to be treated well. Sex is central in this campaign of love bombing because it is inextricably wound up in love and intimacy in your mind. Accordingly, sex is a fundamental aspect of our seduction and there are various things we will do and say of a sexual nature, which you should be aware of. Before I move on to discuss those various facets of sex in the seduction stage it is necessary to examine the two players who are about to become entangled; you and me.

We will naturally start with me (you knew that would be the case didn't you?). You will of course be familiar with what I am since I am a narcissist. You will have some understanding (especially if you have read my other works) of the way I think and behave. In the context of the sexual seduction, I am focussing on my relationship status when I commence my love bombing of you. In order to draw a target closer to me love bombing will always take place. This love bombing has various forms dependent on the target and the type of connection I want to form with my target. The love bombing will take on of two forms:-

- To draw you to me to a degree in order for you to provide me with fuel. For example, complimenting a stranger on a tube train that her perfume is delightful and then following that up with a compliment about her hairstyle or clothing. I have no desire to draw this closer to me so she becomes an acquaintance or something more, I just want her smile which is an admiring gesture to give me a dollop of fuel;

- To draw you to me to elevate your status so you provide me with even greater amounts of fuel by reason of your promotion. Thus, taking the stranger on the tube train again, I may increase the charm to secure going with a coffee with her and then swapping numbers. I may make her an acquaintance for a time and then increase the love bombing so she becomes an outer circle friend, inner circle friend or even an intimate partner. The dosage of love bombing is measured in order to secure the promotion of this individual within the hierarchy of the fuel index. Inevitably, sex will play a part in this.

Let us examine some of the categories of the hierarchy and how the love bombing works with them.

## The Intimate Partner

I wrote in detail in **Fuel** about the rankings of people based on the proximity of supply of fuel. I have repeated the fuel index again below as it is highly relevant when examining the role of sex in the behaviour of a narcissist.

If I want you to become my Intimate Partner, you will be subjected to the Grand Campaign of Love Bombing. All the stops will be pulled out. You may have been a stranger to me, an acquaintance, friend or colleague (or in some instances even a family member) but that does not matter. I have decided that you and I will become an item. We will become boyfriend and girlfriend, we will going steady, stepping out together, involved. Call it what you will but you will be my Intimate Partner. I want this because the Intimate Partner ranks very high as a source of fuel. I always need an Intimate Partner in order to supply me with this fuel. You will not be surprised to find that they will overlap. As I am discarding one, I will be teeing up and drawing in a new one. In order to secure, this very precious supply of fuel I must blitzkrieg you into submission and therefore the love bombing draws on every method of manipulation available to me, it is sustained and incessant.

## The Intermittent Appliance

You will know this person as a booty call or a friend with benefits. We know that person as the Intermittent Appliance. We do not want a relationship with this person but we do want to be able to pick them up when we want and obtain a delicious blast of fuel from them. For one night only (or an afternoon maybe), the Intermittent Appliance will be elevated to the status of an Intimate Partner in order to harvest this fuel. Once this is done they will then revert to the position of Outer Circle Friend who will be kept dangling with the promise of another night of exceptional passion. In order to create someone as an Intermittent Appliance we again must engage in our love bombing. We do not subject the target to a sustained campaign, as we do not want them as an Intimate Partner. Instead, we give them a concentrated dose of love bombing, for example in the early part of the evening, in order to lure them to bed and sink our hooks into them later. We will lay on the charm and the pleasantries and ramp up our sexual overtures in order to move you into bed give you a mind-blowing night and then move away again so you are left dangling. We keep doing this and keep you hanging with the promise of a promotion to become our Intimate Partner. This may in some instances happen or we just keep you dangling, calling on you as and when we need a hit from your fuel and in order to use you to triangulate with our current Intimate Partner.

## The Outer Circle Friend/ Inner Circle Friend

We will take strangers, acquaintances and colleagues and subject them to a lower dose of love bombing (lower compared to the love bombing which creates the above two categories of target but it is still potent) in order to draw you to us so you become an Outer Circle Friend or Inner Circle Friend. Sex will not be involved in this per se, but there will be the potential of sex at some future point and there will be a mild flirtation involved in order to maintain your interest. The point is that love bombing is involved.

## Strangers, Minions, Acquaintances, Colleagues and Family Members

All of these categories of target will be subjected to some form of love bombing. We may use the love bombing to promote them to a new category or just to cause them to provide us with fuel. Examples will include-

- Complimenting a stranger about their looks to receive a thank you and a smile

- Flirtation with the lady who serves me my morning tea every day in the café close to where I work to draw a reaction which gives me fuel

- Complimenting a supplier on their work and praising the standard of their service so they thank me and do something in return for me, both of which give me fuel

- Flirting with a colleague or lauding their work in terms of discussing a promotion within the work place, their response will give me fuel

- Demonstrating affection and warmth to a family member so their response gives me fuel and they remain close to me.

Sex is not always involved in this love bombing but each category of target is subjected to a form of love bombing to either draw fuel or create a new class of target for them which will in turn give me a better quality of fuel. Everyone I come into contact with will be subjected to some form of love bombing. It may be a short and concentrated dose, a low dosage on the odd occasion or a shock and awe campaign of overwhelming love bombing. We must do this and since we are no respecters of boundaries, we regard every person as a target to be subjected to some form of love bombing.

In undertaking this love bombing our status is of little relevance to us. It is unusual to find us single because we like to have an Intimate Partner in place in order to provide us with a steady and reliable source of fuel. Our use of sex in the seduction stage occurs irrespective of our relationship status. We will most likely be seeing somebody, engaged or married when we pick a target and use sex as a means to lure him or her in and provide us with additional fuel. We have no qualms about doing this. When we have set our sights on you as a target, we do not let the fact that we are already apparently committed to someone else stand in the way of our seduction of you. We are able to do this for several reasons:-

- Our need for fuel overrides all other considerations;

- The boundaries that society puts in place with regards to fidelity and monogamy do not apply to us. We are above such restrictions because of our superiority;

- We are entitled to gather fuel. This means we are entitled to seek it from other people and to use sex to do so;

- We are no troubled by a conscience. This has been stripped from us in our development to enable us to gather fuel more readily. The way we have been created is to ensure that we are as efficient as possible at gathering fuel and accordingly all redundant and irrelevant mechanisms such as remorse, guilt and conscience have been removed;

- The fact we may upset our existing partner does not trouble us for the reasons outlined in the point above. Moreover, their upset at learning at our infidelity provides us with a basis for fuel.

Accordingly, our relationship status will never prevent us from using sex during the seduction stage in order to allow us to gather fuel. If our target happens to know that, we are in a relationship and comments on it we will be dismissive. We might have left the house telling you how wonderful you are and that you are the one for us. One hour later, we will be flirting with someone and using our charm on him or her. This charm will invariably be allied with two other elements

- Castigating our existing partner; and

- Playing the victim card

I recall when I was in a relationship with Sarah. We did not live together but I spent most of my time at her house and embarked on doing this from an early point in our coupling. It was after around six months that I found her positive fuel to be waning somewhat. The reduction was not at such a level that caused me undue alarm so I needed to shift to devaluing her in order to open the floodgates on some potent negative fuel. Nevertheless, she was not providing me with the praise and admiration as often as I needed. On one particular occasion, she was occupied in watching one of her favourite television shows, a long running soap which I had absolutely no interest in. Her attention was fixed on the invented day-to-day activities of a group of fictional characters when it should have been focussed on me. I decided I needed some attention elsewhere and told her I was going out. She nodded and said she would see me later, not looking away from the large television set on the wall. I did not take kindly to this at all. I was clearly not interesting enough for her. This ignited my fury and I walked off deciding that I would shield myself from her disgusting implied criticism of me and hunt down some additional fuel. I decided that I would call on Sarah's friend, Joanne who lived nearby. As I slipped on my coat and walked out of the house, I telephoned Joanne.

"Hi HG, what's happening?" she asked brightly. I always liked Joanne. She was pleasant and we got along well. I did not know her before I got with Sarah but whenever I was with her I was the epitome of politeness and urbane charm so she became an Outer Circle Friend.

"Hi Joanne, sorry to disturb you," I said feigning a dismal voice. Joanne was a good empath and I knew she would pick up on my tone straight away and she did.

"What's wrong, you sound upset?"

"Oh I am having problems with Sarah again, could I come round? I need some space. I have tried talking to her but she would rather watch the television."

"Yes sure, sure, are you on your way?" she asked.

"Yes I will be with you in ten minutes."

I was soon at Joanne's and ensconced in her living room with the proverbial nice cup of tea nestling in between my hands. She sat alongside me and adopted a pose of concern. I was already feeling better from this attention that I was receiving from Joanne, the sting of Sarah's criticism beginning to fade. I launched into a tale of woe about how I had been doing so much for Sarah (all of which Joanne knew about because Sarah had been telling her how wonderful I had been helping her move into her new house). I explained that now she was in the house she seemed as if she was not bothered about me and was happier going to work and watching television every night. Joanne defended her friend, as I expected she would do so, by saying that Sarah was keen on me and repeated some of the comments that Sarah had made. This was all good fuel. She did however concede that Sarah could become withdrawn and retreat into a shell. I protested how this is what she was doing but she gave no explanation for her behaviour and it was hurtful. I laid it on thick saying she was no longer interested in sex that she never cuddled at night like she used to and so on. It was all a fabrication but I could see from Joanne's reaction that she was taking it all in and was sympathetic to my position. She held my hand as I spoke and then slipped an arm around me.

"I am sorry to go on, it just upsets me you know, when you give so much of yourself and you get nothing back." Joanne nodded.

"Anyway, listen to me, going on about myself and I have not even asked you how you are. How are you managing after your break-up with Mark?"

I naturally knew about this because of Sarah's regular updates on the saga of Joanne and Mark. It was my turn to appear sympathetic and I let her pour her heart out about that failed relationship. I only really heard one word in four as I was too busy thinking about the fuel I would receive when we kissed. She moved closer the more she spoke until I looked at her, mouths just centimetres apart and I made my move. She responded and we kissed for a few seconds before she broke off.

"We shouldn't you are with Sarah," she reminded.

"I don't think that will last (another lie it went on for a further nine months) and besides I think we both need this don't we?" I pressed.

She gave a small nod.

"She is my friend, we shouldn't."

"I am not going to tell if you won't? Here we are, two upset people who just want to push the pain away, even if it just for a short while. We can forget the world beyond the window and just enjoy this moment. Is that such a bad thing?"

"I understand but you practically live with Sarah," she protested although there was little force in what she said.

"Not at all, I stay over occasionally, it is not as if we are husband and wife is it?" I asked as I kissed her neck.

"Well no, but all the same...."

I placed my finger on her lips.

"We both need this. I have always liked you Joanne but never wanted to say anything in case you felt differently. That kiss just then told me everything that I needed to know. You feel for me the way I feel for you. We cannot fight it. It would be wrong to fight it. We need one another."

She looked me square in the eyes as I maintained my gaze of false sincerity and then she kissed me and I knew I had breached her defences. I took her to bed and it was glorious. Or rather, the fuel she offered me from her urgent mouth and delighted expressions of euphoria as I had her twice. Afterwards I rolled out the speech I often used when engaged in an extra-relationship liaison and she held tight against me. I lay back smiling as I drank in the fuel from her and silently congratulated her on becoming an Intermittent Appliance. Half an hour later, I was back at Sarah's and telling her about the evening I had around at Ian's house. She suspected nothing and her ignorance as I sat there with Joanne's taste still on my lips felt fantastic.

This is just one example of many whereby the fact we are in some form of relationship with another person never proves any kind of hindrance or bar to us using sex in our love bombing, not matter how brief and fierce of another. I had repeated sexual encounters with Joanne but never embarked on a formal relationship with her. Once I decided that Sarah was becoming of less use to me after a prolonged period of denigration I made a move on Kay with the intention of her becoming my Intimate Partner (which she eventually did become). The fact I was still in a relationship with Sarah and infrequently taking to Joanne to bed as well proved no obstacle to my seduction of Kay, but that is a story for another time. The point is that when we are engaging in a sexual liaison with you in order to seduce you, the fact we are already in a relationship is usually a given. This status will never stop us from doing what we want in terms of seducing you. We will do it time and time again. Should you be aware of our status and you willingly engage in an affair with us, we will of course denigrate our current partner by way of explanation for our infidelity. You will be so overcome by our love bombing and the quality of the sex that we give you, that you will have no qualms about being the other woman. Often I keep it quiet but in instances where the target knows I am in a relationship or I have admitted it, the target has never baulked at being the other woman. The power of the seduction and especially the heavenly sex I give that person is so powerful that all thoughts of sisterly solidarity are thrown from the window. Accordingly, our apparent commitment to someone will never stop us from having sex outside of that relationship, whether that person is our girlfriend, partner, co-habitee, fiancée or wife. The use of sex is so powerful in our seduction of you we cannot dismiss it as a weapon. It always has to be used.

Accordingly, in terms of the two participants in the seduction stage that is where we stand but what about you? What status do you have and does this matter to us? It does. The most important status you must have is of being an empathic individual and we can always sense you, work you out and detect you. There are many, many empathic people in the world and you are our prime target. Our kind must seduce you empathic people and naturally, we will use sex as our prime weapon to do this. This is where your status becomes of particular interest to us.

## In a Relationship

If we learn that you are in a relationship with somebody then we want you even more. Why is this? I am sure you have already guessed the answer. It is of course because of the fuel provided. Before I elaborate on that, I will address a point, which may have formed in your mind. You may be familiar with the fact that our kind is keen advocates of preserving energy. This is why we prefer to use words over actions because they are easier to use and use less energy. Accordingly, you may be thinking that trying to lure somebody who is already taken will use up more energy. Our love bombing may have to be more intense, repeated more often and over a longer period of time. This will use up more of our energy but the prospective gains in terms of fuel are such that we will readily expend this additional energy in order to gain the enhanced pay off in fuel. We do not respect the fact you are in a relationship since we do not recognise boundaries. You will provide us with more fuel and there our inflated sense of entitlement means we have to have this fuel. It is our right. We may not realise when we have set our sights on you that you are attached to somebody else. Once we do find this out however we are not dissuaded we are in fact delighted by this revelation.

The resistance you may put up (and believe me not everyone who is in a relationship puts up some resistance, you may be surprised at those who welcome me with near open arms) provides us with fuel. Your verbal protests, your gestures of defensiveness and discomfort at our relentless pursuit all provides us with fuel and encouragement. If the target shows total indifference to us or is uninterested then this will not provide us with any fuel, as there is no emotional gesture. In those circumstances, we will double our efforts but if this neutral state persists, we will abandon the pursuit and seek our fuel elsewhere. This rarely happens. The reason being is that the target will not recognise what we are. The target will just think we are cocky, chancing our arm or that we are a cheeky trier. You may react with surprise, amusement, horror, disgust and objection. We do not mind any of these since these are all reactions and they provide us with fuel. The target will not know that a neutral response is the one thing which if maintained will cause us to break off our pursuit. Empaths, being emotional people, will instead respond in a conventional way by displaying some form of emotion and this suits us. We will heighten our love bombing, seize on any information you provide us that demonstrates any form of dissatisfaction with your current partner, no matter how small in order to drive a wedge between you and him. We will turn all our seduction dials up to the maximum and we will keep drawing on your fuel until we seduce you. No means nothing to us.

Often the excitement of engaging in an affair proves a tantalising inducement to our target, especially if they have some form of dissatisfaction with their current partner. They have a void in their life and we know how to fill it with our seductive words, which are sent in mid-morning texts, whispered telephone calls and clandestine e-mails. We are the best person to conduct an affair with because we conduct so many ourselves we achieve the status of an expert and can guide you through your own affair with ease. This masterful approach also proves very alluring to you. You love the intense and frenetic sexual encounters, in the back of cars, in motel rooms, behind buildings and the like. You find it intoxicating because we make it intoxicating. In the same way, we draw someone in who is single through our dizzying application of love bombing, of which sex is an integral part, the fact you are doing something you should not actually ends up making it easier for us to keep you drawn to us. We may face resistance when we begin our seduction of you, but the fuel you give us sustains us as we expend our energy, but once we have broken you so that you yield to us, the exciting element of conducting an affair actually makes it easier for us to keep you bound to us. Knowing that we have overcome your initial resistance means that the fuel you provide to us once you have succumbed is especially sweet.

We also like the fact you are in a relationship because it means that once we have ensnared you, you want to get in touch with us. We do not have to do much work to keep you interested. The hidden nature of the affair also means that this provides us with additional time to find fuel from other sources since we cannot be with you all the time. More often than not, we will be conducting an affair anyway but if we are not and perhaps we are between relationships, with a number of ongoing dating prospects, connecting with several lovers through the auspices of an affair is especially appealing to us. It adds to the fuel and gives us a particular sense of omnipotence.

A further advantage of conducting an affair and being the other man is of course your existing partner. Whilst I am screwing you senseless he is sat at home oblivious and this makes me feel powerful. There is also the prospect of him finding out. Indeed, in certain instances I will allow us to be caught so there is a fantastic reaction from the injured party. Do I care that I am shouted at, threatened and called all the names under the sun? Not one jot. This is even more fuel. The chaotic scene as he discovers us engaged in oral sex in your car provides me with a massive fuel boost. Imagine the scene as he bangs on the window.

"What the fuck is going on here?" he yells face contorted in rage. You lift your head from my lap and give a gasp of horror as you see your boyfriend looking down at you.

"What's the problem?" I ask knowing only too well, what it is.

"What's the problem? That's my bloody girlfriend whose mouth is clamped around your dick, you bastard."

"Richard please, please calm down," you beg as he pulls on the car door. I sit and look at him as he slams his hands against the window.

"Your girlfriend? Really? She never said," I smile pleasantly.

"You fucking whore," he erupts and marches around to the passenger door.

"HG what do I do?" you ask looking at me with those earnest and pleading eyes. The fuel is flowing well here.

"Not my problem, you never said you had a boyfriend," I answer in a typical riposte of blame shifting and denial of responsibility.

"I did, you knew about him, I told you about him," you say quickly as Richard pulls on the passenger door.

"No I don't think you did," I answer flatly staring at the irate boyfriend and then looking back at your disbelieving face.

"Hg?" you wail.

"I think someone wants to talk to you," I note and motion to Richard as he continues to pound on the door.

"He will kill me, finding us like this, how did he know?"

"No idea but you didn't tell me you had a boyfriend, you shouldn't have done that, you are out of order," I declare narrowing my eyes.

"I did, I certainly did," you start to cry as you look over your shoulder.

"Help me, please, he will kill me," you beg.

"Oh no, you are just a dirty whore, you are not dragging me into your domestic mess," I say and press the door lock. The door is opened and the car is filled with the angry shouts of Richard as he grabs you by the arm.

"HG please," you beg as he hauls you out of the car, tears streaming down your face. He pulls you away as I reach across and slam the door shut. Richard turns and makes for the door but I press the lock again and he stands impotent mouthing insults at me. I see you behind him, cowed and frightened as I give you both a wave and drive off fuel splashing all over me. Fantastic.

You may be wondering whether I have been hunted down by a jealous partner who wishes to exact some revenge on me. Of course, I have and I use my charm to diffuse the situation, apportion all the blame on to you and escape from the situation unscathed. I will admit there have been a few close shaves but I always manage to get out of the situation and leave you and him to pick up the pieces. Even after detection and the subsequent explosion, I am perfectly content to come back for more. You may have been cast aside by your partner and therefore your relief at being able to continue with me is huge and rewarding and means you are especially prone to be manipulated into doing what I want. Even if you patch things up, I will have another crack at you. You have tasted the heavenly nectar of being entangled with our kind and you will want more. No matter what promises you have made to be faithful, I will have you again because you want it to so badly. You may deem this as arrogant and despicable behaviour. Feel free to tell me this, it is all fuel.

## **Married**

All of the above is applicable and it is heightened by virtue of the fact that society places such sanctity on this institution of marriage. The reaction from both you and your cuckolded spouse becomes maximised as a consequence of this increased status and in turn, this furnishes me with greater degrees of fuel. The fact that a target presents as married makes that target even more inviting. Indeed the fact that the target is married tells me that that person is most empathic as they have sworn themselves to cherish and care for one person and they most likely have been doing this repeatedly. I also know that the way your long-term relationships evolve is that they settle into routine, similar behaviours and ultimately boredom comes creeping in. This is a fertile ground onto which I can sow my seeds of dazzling excitement, shiny attraction and mesmerising seduction and reap the rewards. The attention I shall pay you from my love bombing will seem like such a refreshing change that no matter what resistance you might put up.

You may think that is mainly men that are predatory creatures who will break their wedding vows for a night of illicit extra-marital sex. Believe me there are plenty and I mean plenty of women who behave in a similar way. Where do I find them? Dating sites and chat rooms. They are crawling with people who are misbehaving because they think that the internet provides them with some degree of anonymity and also the opportunity to present a false self in the hope of proving attractive to someone. There are the female of my kind prowling around these electronic honeypots and I will spot them a mile off and avoid them, even if I knew I could defeat them and make them mine. Too much effort and not enough fuel. There are those, which are just sex hungry and are not empathic so I root those out and dismiss them. Amongst those two categories, however there are plenty of bored married women who are just dipping a toe in the water by having a chat. They do not seriously intend to be unfaithful it is just that they do not receive any attention, their beds are barren wastelands and they would like to be shown some affection. Of course, you would and I will give you plenty but once you have responded to my message it is only a question of time before you will be lured into bed with me. It has happened repeatedly. Using my oft-applied salami slicing technique I will chip away, pushing you a little further each time, drawing you closer with my flattery, exuding false sympathy to ascertain what is wrong with your existing relationship and dangling that shiny carrot of charmed seduction in front of you. You always bite and I always catch my prey. Finding these married ladies is very easy and the challenge of seducing them by bedding them is most attractive in terms of the fuel that is garnered.

It also reinforces my superiority. I can have anyone I want. Even the vows of marriage collapse under my unstoppable charm. Before you judge me too harshly, I am only giving them what they yearn for. If they were getting my attention, charm, wit and generosity at home, they would not stray but they are not and they do. I am able to look on the cuckolded husband and scoff at his inferiority to me. I am able to conquer whom I want and vanquish all that oppose me. That is how powerful I am and the sensation is edifying.

## Virgins

This is a category, which is proving particularly rare these days. The concept of the preservation of virginity until wedlock is rather outdated, sadly and given that, I do not engage with someone under the age of twenty-three my exposure to virgins will be particularly limited. This was not always the case. Once upon a time, when I was younger and therefore the 23yr old rule did not apply I was able to find these virgins. There were a surprising number at university and even afterwards, when I commenced my career the office at its large number of employees would throw up the occasional virgin amongst the younger women who worked there. Trish was a girlfriend who was a virgin when I met her. This was at university. Trish was not religious and certainly, no wallflower and she showed no embarrassment at admitting she was a virgin. She did not shout it from the rooftops but when it arose in context, she was content to admit that that was the case. I remember that there was a group of us who were talking about relationships and sex in the pub one day and this was when Trish, who lived in the same college as me but was reading for a different degree, admitted she was a virgin. I worked out that there were at least two lads in the group who were virgins too but of course, they would not admit to that. Trish's admission provoked discussion but I paid little attention to all of that, I was too busy plotting how I would seduce her because the thought of conquering this virgin territory was massively appealing. Back then I was not familiar with the effect of gaining fuel, I just knew that people praising me, wanting me and giving me attention made me feel powerful. I knew that doing what I wanted, when I wanted and how I wanted had a similar effect. By taking Trish's virginity, I knew I would feel powerful. She was not averse to other forms of sexual contact so it was not a complete no-go area, not that I cared. Whether I masturbated myself or she did it, the physical sensation was entirely the same. It was her sighs and cries of delight when I used my fingers and tongue on her sweet, silky heaven that I wanted. The fact that I had to use my mouth and fingers alone to achieve her climaxes meant there was a challenge and it was one I readily accepted and the reaction was satisfying. It also maintained my interest along with the ultimate aim of deflowering her. It was after a year of being with her by being charming attentive and a "good" boyfriend that she finally felt ready to give herself to me. I was no a virgin. Far from it and the prospect of taking her virginity and the power associated with that (or as I later learned the fuel that would arise from it) was most exciting.

The evening of the act, itself was straight out of the romance novels. A lovely dinner, a walk by the river and then back to my digs where in the candle lit we undressed as we had many times before only this time the last piece of her clothing would be removed as she shed her virginity. Applying my practised technique, I aroused her as I had previously although her nervousness did make it difficult. This was one of the few times I was persuaded to wear a condom since she vowed she would not allow me to have her unless I wore one. I agreed, the annoyance at having to do so falling second to the outcome of deflowering her. I could tell she did not enjoy it and it hurt her. That was to be expected. There was no heavenly orgasm for her but rather an embarrassed shrug after I had faked my own climax (I grew bored and her reaction was causing me to lose my erection) so I faked the deed and darted to the toilet to remove the condom before she could see it was empty. When I returned, I felt annoyance rather than powered delight since there was no admiration and I felt the urge to lash out and to be cruel to her, berating her for her failure to climax despite my best endeavours (which always worked). She looked up at me and smiled holding out her hands towards me. I took them and she pulled me in towards her. She held me close and whispered into my ear,

"It does not matter that I didn't come, you always make me anyway, what mattered was having you inside me. I love you so much and you are my first. It is on a spiritual level that I came because we joined together and became as close as two people can ever get." I looked at her and the first tear of happiness trickled from her right eye. Her emotional reaction immediately removed the annoyance and irritation that she had caused to rise and instead I felt the power washing over me at how I had moved her on a spiritual level. It sounded like nonsense but I could see in her eyes that it truly meant something to her, despite the physical discomfort and pain. I never forgot those words and I have trotted them out, or a variation of them myself when the occasion required it. The effect I felt from taking Trish's virginity and the journey towards doing so were both worthwhile and ever since the virginal empath is high on my list of targets.

It was a bountiful time during university, tracking down those virgins and accepting the challenge to seduce them and deflower them with what I now know to be the attendant fuel flowing from them. The heady power that arose from a triumphant conquest certainly paved the way for me wanting to do it again although of course with the progress of time the opportunities to find the challenge of a virgin for seduction have been reduced. It is worth mentioning someone else in this section by way of demonstration of how a challenging relationship status on your part proves particularly alluring to us. This involved Gemma.

When I embarked on my postgraduate course, I moved into a house with my best friend at the time, Paul. There were already two people living in the house when we took our tenancy. The first was a lad called Steven. Pleasant chap, willowy with very white-blonde hair and who seemed in a permanent state of anxiety. Particularly studious but amenable enough. There was also Gemma. Dear Gemma. She was the walking embodiment of miserableness. I recall when I would rise early and would be eating breakfast she would shuffle; she never walked properly, into the dining room and would wave lethargically at me. Apparently, I later learned, she was always too tired to talk first thing in the morning. Not that I cared. She always had bags under her eyes, a resigned expression on her face and lank, centre-parted long hair, which was a dull dark brown with grey already appearing. She was pale with a slim yet somehow doughy figure, which arose from the fact that she was sitting in an armchair, sitting in a car or sitting in a lecture theatre. The one day she decided to walk into college, she moaned for three days afterwards that it had left her stiff. Gemma was engaged to Christopher. He was a good-looking in a boyish way, chap from Northern Ireland. He did not live with us but across the city and was a fairly regularly fixture calling across to see Gemma a few times a week. He would occasionally stay over as well. I remember when he first introduced himself with a winning smile as Gemma's fiancé that I was taken aback. She was certainly punching above her weight in being engaged to him. He was lively, chirpy and attractive. She was a raincloud. I wondered how on earth they were together and it soon became clear. First of all God had united them. They were committed Christians. Second and probably more importantly, Gemma came from money. Lots of money. Old Ulster Boy had hit the financial jackpot with her and he was obviously willing to put up with staring at misery guts in order to lay his hands on the cash. I did not begrudge him this. He deserved it. I also suspected that his devoutness was based on cosying up to her, something that I later exploited. In the course of an evening discussion we happened on to the topic of sex and both Gemma and Christopher admitted with glee they were both virgins and they were waiting until they were married. Not only that but the only thing they ever did was kiss. They did not even sleep in the same bed when Christopher stayed over. He would sleep on an airbed on the floor. I tried not to laugh; I had heard the airbed being pumped up and mistakenly thought they were engaged in coitus. I was very wrong.

Learning of this arrangement however was just too good an opportunity to miss. At the time, I marvelled at how much power I would gain from throwing a spanner into this set-up. Should I corrupt him, her, or both? I felt dizzy at the prospect. I had my own girlfriend at the time and she was based two hundred miles to the north so I saw her every now and again. I occupied myself with the other women at the university and in the city but here was a prospect that I could not let pass. I had 9 months to weave my dark magic and I set to work. I feigned interest in their religion and spent numerous occasions say discussing it with Gemma. Her admiration for my questions and understanding provided me with decent fuel as I salami-sliced my way into her affections. I would not relay messages from Christopher when he called so that their arrangements would be messed up and deny ever speaking to him. Gemma would rather blame him than her new disciple. I enlisted the help of a friend to whisper poison in Christopher's ear about Gemma and to lead him astray in the bars. I would then on some pretext be out and about with Gemma and just happen upon Christopher who would be drunk, something she disliked. She would become upset and I would comfort her as little by little I drove a wedge between them and embedded myself in her affections. The whole process merits a volume to the insidious way in which I wormed my way into her bed and had her after six months of sterling effort. Previously untouched she was a firecracker and the dour and miserable demeanour vanished as one drunken evening she finally succumbed. Her ecstatic reaction was fantastic and I truly was a master of seduction. Not only had I taken her virginity, I had taken it from someone who had kept it for a compelling reason and whilst betrothed to another. It was a trinity of triumphs. She was wracked with guilt the next day and made me swear not to say anything to Christopher. I did not say anything because I was pleased that I had a huge piece of leverage to use against her.

That was a memorable conquest and again demonstrated just how attractive and alluring someone who is deemed as unattainable is to someone like me when I am using sex to seduce.

I have continued my hunt for those of a virginal persuasion and thanks to Gemma and her religious instruction; I occasionally bear fruit by dipping into the pool of empaths at a local church. I savour the challenge of finding the suitable target and then deflowering them. It has been some time since I had one and I suspect that I may need to cast my net wider to find a result but I know there are more out there. The non-virgin empaths I find at church are a delight and they also provide a challenge since they tend to lead lives, which are, shall we say, of greater moral upstanding. They take their marriage vows seriously and are not ones to be seen to be "putting it about". The twin challenge of religion and attachment to another is also most inviting. I am encouraged of course by the fact that the nuns in *The Devils* gave in to lewd and licentious behavious so even the religious types are not immune to the lure of the devil.

## **Frigidity**

Another challenge in selecting a target for my use of sex in the seduction stage is the person who is afflicted by frigidity, or, as I prefer to regard it as the person who just has not met me yet. Now, nobody, or at least nobody I have met admits to being frigid. They may express a lack of interest in sex or be disdainful about certain sexual practices but they do not tend to admit that they are frigid. I soon learned however that the way to find these targets is to listen to the barroom complaints of their other halves.

"We never have sex any more, she just isn't interested."

"She gives the garden more attention than me."

"I try every Friday and it is always the same, she is too tired or too stressed."

"I have given up. I just wank and watch porn now."

"She doesn't want it. She never had much of a sex drive as it was and it has completely petered out."

I nod sympathetically when I hear these Acquaintances, Family Members and Outer Circle friends bemoans their lack of action. This is a flashing light to me that their other half is suffering from frigidity or at least she is with the oaf she has shacked up together in their home. Attracted by the twin allure of the target being frigid and attached, along with the prospect of gaining fuel from two sources, I soon set to work in order to achieve my goal. The energy expended in breaking down her barriers and using sex to seduce her is easily rewarded by the satisfying fuel that is obtained and the feeling of power accompanying it.

## **Lesbians**

Of course, I am a subscriber to the belief that they can be turned. Anyone can be turned. It is just a matter of knowing the right things to say and do. Sexuality is just a sliding scale. Some people prefer their own sex nearly all the time, some people prefer the opposite sex nearly all the time and then there is a vast place in between. How many men become aroused at watching lady boy porn? How many of them watch a transgender person engage in sex with a man and woman and find it stimulates them? How about hermaphrodites? Bisexuals are just greedy of course because it doubles their chances on a Saturday night, but sexuality is a sliding scale.

Again, I prefer women, I touch on the issue of homosexuality later in this book, but my choice of appliance for an intimate partner is a woman. Some of my kind who are male will choose a man. Who cares as long as you are getting fuel? I know that I am structured to obtain the best fuel from a member of the opposite sex and therefore that is why I choose to seduce them with sex. It might be different in another world for me but it is not, so women it is. This means of course that in terms of finding empathic targets, which prove a challenge, lesbians enter the picture as well. Some may have had sexual experiences with men because society expected them to be heterosexual before they then found their natural place with lesbianism. Others may have been raised in an environment, which gave them a push towards lesbianism, such as an all-girls school. They enjoyed some teenage experimentation and enjoyed the Sapphic encounters and have stuck with it ever since. Others may have had a lesbian period at school and then left that behind. The influence of the environment can have that effect. I think it was Robert Graves in his book *Goodbye to All That* when he remarked about homosexuality in British private education he wrote that,

"For every one true homosexual there were ten pseudo-homosexuals."

Thus, some of the products of single sex education may be latent heterosexuals, something I believe in as it provides me with the incentive to seduce a lesbian. I have had three successes in this arena. I must admit alcohol played a part in two of the successes but they were entirely aware and consenting, they were just more amenable to my overtures after quaffing a bottle and a half of Chablis. Once again conquering those, which would ordinarily be deemed off limits, provided me with a tremendous degree of fuel.

It is worth making the point that with this empathic challenge target it is not necessarily the case that we want them as our Intimate Partner. More often than not, they are an Intermittent Appliance or even a one-off. In the last case, it is akin to conquering a mountain. It had to be done, I have triumphed and it feels great but there is no need to climb that particular mountain again in respect of that person. I will find someone else in his or her challenge category and look to conquer him or her and again as a one off but conquer him or her I must. Sex is the absolute key to these challenges because their supposed lack of availability is always linked to sex.

- The person in a relationship is expected to be faithful

- The married individual has given vows of fidelity

- The virgin has deemed penetrative sexual intercourse as forbidden

- The frigid woman has deemed sex as off limits

- The lesbian has declared heterosexual sex to be off limits

- The religious person may deem sex off limits

In each instance, sex remains the key element to their apparently unobtainable state. By using sex during my seduction of them, the reward is all the greater.

Thus in ascertaining the target for our sexual seduction, we want an empath first and foremost. The empath will fit into any of the categories of proximity of source, which I have described and will often end up being an intimate partner. In continuing with our use of sex as a way to seduce and gain fuel, we will also look for other targets, which are deemed as challenges. These are prime considerations in our behaviour and our quest for fuel.

## The Role of Sex in the Seduction Stage

Having established that sex is a prime weapon of the somatic or the elite narcissist and why this is the case and furthermore having considered how the status of both you and me affects this dynamic, it falls to examine how this weapon is used. As you are familiar, we operate in a cycle of seduction, devaluation, discard and re-seduction (Hoovering). Sex appears in all of these stages and does so in a fundamental fashion, which it is necessary for you to understand. We start with how the narcissist uses sex in the seduction stage. The key objectives of sex in the seduction stage are as follows:-

- The creation of premium quality fuel

- A means of drawing you closer to us

- A means of keeping you close to us

- A means of creating something to be used against you

- A means of control

I suggest you read these again because they will feature in everything that we do when we are using sex to seduce you. Whether it is the issue of contraception, the tenderness that we show towards you when we bed you or the heightened sex drive we have, the above considerations will be applicable. Similarly, if you think that our seduction is based on the following:-

- Our love for you

- Our attraction to you in terms of how you look and/or your interests

- Our desire to make you happy

You could be forgiven for believing this because we will want you to believe this. We will create an illusion encompassing these things. The reality is none of that applies. What really applies is-

- Our love of the fuel you give us;

- Our attraction to you in terms of how you provide us with fuel;

- Our desire to make you happy so you give us fuel.

In the book **Fuel,** I describe the fuel index, which is based on how we grade the fuel that you provide. This is calculated by reference to the proximity of the supply and the method of delivery. It is worth referring to the proximity of source once again for the purposes of understanding how we use sex during the seduction. The list starts with the lesser valued source rising to the most valued.

# Proximity of the Source

Remote strangers

Strangers

Minions

Acquaintances

Colleagues

Outer Circle Friends

Inner Circle Friends

Family

Intimate Partners

Former Intimate Partners (devalue "DV")

Former Intimate Partners (hoover ("H"))

Take a look at this list. The narcissist draws fuel from all of these groups and will often do so in one day alone such is the thirst for this fuel. There will be a primary source of fuel, which is usually an intimate partner, and the other sources provide additional fuel. Our kind will draw fuel from any of these sources in the context of using sex as a mechanism. Look through that list again. Our kind will have sex with strangers, friends, colleagues, intimate partners and even family members for drawing fuel. Incest does occur but typically, the use of a family member might be a sister-in-law for example or the sister of a girlfriend.

There are varying methods of delivery, which are also ranked. The negative methods of delivery provide the most potent fuel but we will be addressing that in a later chapter. Here we are concerned with six types of methods of delivery, which arise from sex. In ascending order they are

Loving Gestures
Loving Words
Attentive Gestures
Attentive Words
Admiring Gestures
Admiring Words

In the overall scheme of fuel, these six elements rank from fifth to tenth and are essentially the upper middle through to the lower middle of methods of delivery. Note how admiration ranks above loving. That is why after we have made love to you we like to hear

"I love you so much"

But we would much rather hear

"That was amazing, you are brilliant."
We hold admiring praise in higher esteem than love. This runs contrary to what you would do. Our aim is to use sex to obtain these responses and preferably admiring gestures and admiring words from a whole host of sources. Amongst those sources in the seduction, stage we want to draw this fuel from intimate partners most of all. This is why we move with unseemly haste to establish a relationship with you. To you, you may regard being in a relationship something that happens after three to four months of dating. To us we regard it as a relationship based on calling you our girlfriend, being engaged or married to you, getting you pregnant, moving in together. If we move in after two weeks to us that is a relationship. This moves you from acquaintance or outer circle friend to intimate partner. This means the positive fuel you will give through the above methods of delivery arising from sex will be of a better quality sooner. We are therefore always in a rush to get you into a relationship status through the above measures so we regard you as an intimate partner.

In order to obtain fuel we want you entranced by our performance. We know we are brilliant but we want you to show us and/or tell us. We want to hear the panting breaths, the cries for more and for us to keep going and we want to see your face contorted in delight. We need to hear your cries of ecstasy we want you to tell us how good it feels, how we are the best and how nobody else has ever done this. Feed us this throughout. Tell us that you love us, tell us how close you feel to us, and shout out that this is fucking amazing. Give it to me, give it to me, give it to me. It is all about your appreciation of how good we are. We love to know how we performed and we will frequently ask

"How was it for you?"
"How did that make you feel?"
"Feel better now?"
"How was that?"

You will not notice this at the time because you are too wrapped up the love bombing but one of our red flags is the repeated questioning of you about how you found our sexual encounter. We will invariably ask you during sex how you are finding it and afterwards as well. We will make repeated references to it away from the bedroom as well. Look out for comments and questions such as there:-

"Last night was great wasn't it?"
"I really enjoyed making love to you, did you?"
"What do you like best when we are in bed together?"
"Did you like it when I did x/y and/or z?"
"How intense was your orgasm last night?"
"You really seemed to be getting into it last night, yes?"
"Have you always made so much noise when having sex?"

All of this is naturally engineered to cause you to give us feedback. We know that empathic individuals would rarely want to hurt someone's feelings and this is especially so when dealing with a sensitive subject such as sex. We also know that we are good at it so we ask these questions knowing we will receive positive replies and thus this allows us to gather additional fuel. What else can you expect when we are using sex to seduce you?

**Spontaneous Sex**

We like to surprise you with this because it will cause you to give an immediate reaction of surprised delight, which fuels us. This is not confined to penetrative sex however and will involve touching and oral sex without any warning. You might be chopping vegetables in the kitchen and we will come in behind you and begin to kiss your neck and run our hands all over you. You will not reject this advance because you are very much in the golden period of our relationship when we are smothering you with affection and desire. You feel wanted and it is exciting to be approached suddenly and without warning. You are not exasperated to be stopped from doing your task but instead you yield and join in. We do this repeatedly as we have no recognition of any boundaries. You are with us and we will lay our hands on your whenever we want and wherever we like. We will grope you on public transport, in the car, sat at home watching a film, in the cinema, at a restaurant and so on. You will believe that this is being done because we are so attracted to you that we cannot literally keep our hands off you. The reality is that we are doing this to make you feel wanted. We are creating the impression that you are highly desirable to us. In one respect you are but not in the way that you think. You are highly desirable to us because of the fuel that you provide. We paw and grope you because we expect you to provide us with a favourable reaction. We will suddenly turn up and whisk you away for mid-afternoon sex. You will think it is wonderful that we are so spontaneous and always ready to take you to bed. We are anything but. We plan this so-called spontaneity to ensure we are doing the following:-

- Reinforcing your connection to us
- Gathering fuel from you
- Making you dependent on us

You raise no objection to this behaviour as you have been conditioned to think that it is fun, exciting and shows how much we want you. It is a flagrant breach of your boundaries. We regard you as ours. You are an appliance to us. You are an object. We can press the button in order to extract fuel from you and we expect it. By kneading you, prodding you, touching you and caressing you we will elicit the appropriate reaction. The sudden nature of this behaviour will seem exciting to you and framed within the love bombing that we have been subjecting you to; you will always oblige and yield to our advances.

**Public Sex**

We are huge exhibitionists. We love to show off and we do not regard normal conventions as applicable to us. We are special and entitled to do as we please. You belong to us, you are our appliance and therefore we expect you to go along with what we want (this foreshadows a darker side which we will visit during the devaluation). You can expect us to initiate sex and for it to take place in a public location. This will often be combined with the spontaneity described above. If you have any reluctance to doing this, we will keep on at you, flattering you and gently cajoling you until you agree. You will also not want to be seen as a stick in the mud and our subtle manipulation of you ensures you will go along with it. We are also sowing the seeds for a later more nefarious use of this exhibitionism. By conditioning you to indulge in it at this seduction stage, we will then turn it to our advantage in a more disturbing fashion at a later stage.

There are various forms of exhibitionism. For my part, I prefer to undertake it with a partner because I want the maximum amount of fuel. I want a reaction from the intimate partner (or outer circle friend acquaintance or stranger that I am with) and from those who witness what we are doing. It will not always be about penetrative sex with you. It is all about getting a reaction from both you and those who witness the exhibitionism. Some examples of this will include:-

We ensure that you are not wearing any underwear underneath a short skirt. I will position you to sit opposite a man and essentially do a Sharon Stone in Basic Instinct. I find this one works very well in departure lounges at airports because of the angle of the seating and the availability of plenty of seats facing one another. A high stool in a bar works as well. You go along with it because you get a sexual thrill from it and you want to impress me. I will have reassured you by saying I will make love to you afterwards and you will find it exhilarating. I have also explained that you cannot get into trouble as the person viewing will like it and if they do not then they will not complain because they will be seen as some kind of pervert for looking. I draw fuel from you becoming excited by doing this, the other person's reaction and your response thereafter. I am also exerting my control over you by getting you to perform this act.

A variation on the above theme will be where I actual expose you by lifting your skirt to show off your bottom or I quickly open your blouse from behind to somebody nearby. Once again, fuel is obtained from your startled excitement at engaging in this, the other person's shocked and delighted reaction and I also assert my control by being the one who decides when the exposure takes place. If I do not do the exposing I will cause you to do the flashing instead as I watch on nearby.

We may engage in mooning which will invariably gain a reaction. I used to moon a lot when I was younger and usually with my friends. From time to time, I would do it when with a girlfriend and her shocked but amused reaction would fuel me. I took this further when I found a particular bar in my city, which had a considerable amount of pedestrian traffic outside.

The windows of the bar were floor to ceiling with a shelf at stomach height all the way along to place drinks etc. I would tell my friends what I was going to do and then unzip my trousers and pull my genitals into the open and leave them hanging there. People would walk past, occasionally notice, point, and stare as I pretended not to know what they were looking at. My friends found this hysterical. Nobody ever complained since the passers-by were invariably young and drunk. I would gain fuel from the reactions of the passers-by and my friends.

I have not done this but streaking is another exhibitionist act that our kind will perform. There is no sexual gratification involved at all. It is all about provoking a reaction from those who witness it. Whenever I have seen a streaker at a major sporting event, I imagine that the fuel must be immense as they hear the shocked shouts, delighted laughs and hoots of approval from sixty thousand spectators. What a fuel dump that must be.

I also get girlfriends to engage in reflectoporn whereby they will stand naked and there will be a reflection say in a toaster, a kettle or a spoon. I will take a picture of the reflection, which will be used for a later occasion (this is discussed in a later chapter), but the act of getting this person to engage in this act is a further form of exhibitionism which draws a positive reaction from you and thus fuel for me.

I am even able to garner a reaction from people from my Sheela na gig. I managed to acquire one from a church when it was undergoing some renovations. If you are unfamiliar with what this is, it is a stone carving of a naked woman displaying an exaggerated vulva. It is a form of gargoyle.

Apparently, they were created to ward off evil spirits but I have it to create a reaction. I have the gig position in my hallway and everyone who enters my house always notices it and invariably provides a shocked reaction upon seeing it. They always ask what it is which gives me a good opportunity to demonstrate my knowledge, as they look on fascinated and open-mouthed. I also use it as a form of suggestion as to what will happen later between the four walls of my home.

When our kind engages in exhibitionism, it is not a sexual act. It is about gaining a reaction and therefore fuel. We will pull the car over in a lay by and expect you to fellate us. We will find a semi-secluded spot and have sex with you. You can expect to have a lot of sex in your garden in the hope that your neighbours see us at it. If you happen to work at the same place as us, we will expect a "quickie" during the lunch break in a storeroom or the disabled toilet or some other spot we can find in the relevant building. On holiday, we will have you on the beach or in the swimming pool. We will bend you over and take you from behind on the balcony, as we look around triumphant that we are no doubt observed from the adjoining hotel. You will find this exciting. The risk of being seen will heighten the excitement for you and more than likely will make the sex feel even better so you have a delicious climax and then praise us for it. The fuel pours from you. You should keep an eye out for the fact than when we are having sex with you in a public place we will be looking around to see if anybody has noticed us. If we catch somebody's eye this will spur us on because his or her reaction be it one of sly admiration or outraged disbelief provides us with a nice dollop of fuel as well. When we are having sex in a public place, you might be thinking something along the lines of-

"This is naughty but my God it is good, he is so exciting, I hope we don't get caught though."

This is what I will be thinking.
"Look at me everyone I am a sexual master of the universe. See how much she is enjoying this and it is all because of me. Look on and marvel at my sexual dominance, I bet you would love some too wouldn't you?"

It is all about the performance and receiving attention for us. We have no qualms about being watched or discovered. In fact, we hope for it to happen as the reaction of others gives us fuel. We have no concern about falling foul of the law because that is just for the little people. Our fuel comes first and in any event should we be approached by a police officer whilst taking you across the bonnet in a picnic area we will just charm that police officer out of taking any action or invite them to join in. There are people who engage in exhibitionism who are not of our kind although I would suggest that those who do are exhibiting a narcissistic tendency even though they are not narcissists. Interestingly, amongst those who engage in exhibitionism a survey ( *Freund, K., Watson, R., & Rienzo, D. (1988) The value of self-reports in the study of voyeurism and exhibitionism*) asked the exhibitionists what their preferred reaction was in the person who witnessed their exhibitionism. The responses were as follows:-

"Would want to have sexual intercourse" (35.1%),
"No reaction necessary at all" (19.5%)

"To show their privates also" (15.1%)

"Admiration" (14.1%)

"Any reaction" (11.9%)

"Anger and disgust" (3.8%)

"Fear" (0.5%)

This demonstrates that most exhibitionists are not narcissists. If you asked a narcissist who engaged in exhibitionism the same question the bottom four responses would be the top ones. We would want admiration, any reaction, anger and disgust and fear because a response equates to fuel.

## Mirrors

As you might expect, mirrors play a part in our sexual profile. This is another form of exhibitionism but merits highlighting. We like to involve mirrors in our sexual congress with people. This is done so we can see your reactions and moreover to see ourselves. In my bedroom I have a full-length mirror which I can move. I will position this when I take someone from behind so that I can see their face. This enables me to focus on their facial expressions so I can see how much they are enjoying themselves, so they can look me in the eye and send me those passionate, desirable and admiring looks. It also enables me to admire myself as I dominate the person I am with, gripping them by the shoulders or pulling at their hair. I can see myself as the titan I am as they are subjugated beneath me.

In one of the spare bedrooms I have built-in wardrobes on each side of the bedroom and these have mirrored doors. I will take my sex partner in this room and have them on the king size bed. The beauty of this room is that I am able to see myself from all angles and moreover there is an infinite number of me reflected in all these mirrors which gives me a huge sense of omnipotence. It is as if I am having sex with thousands upon thousands of people all at one and all of them are looking at me with admiration and desire. The fuel I gain from this is sensational. I am able to admire my technique and my physicality as I make my way through the gears with whoever I have taken into this room. I always smile to myself in this room as it puts me in mind of a scene from one of my favourite films *American Psycho*. For those of you who do not know the film, Patrick Bateman, the central character and very much one of our elite, is engaged in a threesome with a high class escort and a street hooker. He has them positioned as he wants them and as he takes one of them from behind he looks at his reflection, flexing his biceps and winking at himself. I know exactly why he is doing this.

## **Lighting**

During the seduction stage there will always be lighting for the simple reason I must see your face and your reactions. Naturally I will ensure that it is suitable low lit to create the right atmosphere and to assuage any concerns you may have about being seen naked but there must always be sufficient light to allow me to watch your reactions. If you ask for the lights to be out I will pour on the charm about how beautiful you look and how I want to look into your eyes and therefore we need some light. I will be lovely and charming and flatter you into agreeing.

### Pictures and Filming

Once we have drawn you closer to us during the seduction phase we will also want to take pictures of you naked and engaged in sexual acts as well as film you. We will undertake this covertly if necessary but also prefer to gain your consent. This is nothing to do with our concerns for the legality of what we are doing but it is based purely on gaining another reaction from you. We want pictures and film of you engaged in sexual activity for the following reasons:-

- To use against you at a later stage
- To draw a reaction from you now
- To allow us to view them at a later stage and enjoy your reaction again so as to gather fuel and to also appraise our magnificent technique
- To use for the purposes of triangulation

Capturing you in film and picture is not done in a threatening manner during the seduction phase. We continue to exhibit affection, love and charm towards you in order to coerce you gently to go along with it. We will tell you how beautiful you are and how we want to preserve this. We promise they are for our use only and we would never dream of showing them to anybody else. We will express how much we love you and we want to create a permanent record of our wonderful love-making. We may make mention of how a previous girlfriend agreed but of course I deleted all the pictures and film once we split up (this is of course a lie – I have a considerable library which I will touch on in greater detail later). As with many of my manipulative wiles I may start by taking some photographs of you fully clothed and then suggest you show some leg or some shoulder. Little by little, wrapped up in charm and compliments, I will remove each piece of clothing until eventually I have those photographs of you naked, stored and catalogued. If you manage to resist I will film you covertly in any event but I always prefer that you agree with you looking directly into the camera with those fuel-filled eyes.

**Broadcasting**

You can expect during the seduction stage for all and sundry to know about us. This is done for two reasons. To let people know how happy I am with you so you feel honoured and delighted by my broadcasting, which in turn draws you closer to me. It is also to let the person I have recently discarded know that I am with someone new and better so that I can gain fuel from their hurt and angry reaction to this news. This broadcasting takes the form of telling people, getting my Lieutenants to spread the news and most of all frequent and repeated postings through social media. This broadcasting is no different in the sexual arena. We are not crude or lascivious in the way we go about this. There is no need for such conduct as we are maintaining our façade of a being a perfect gentlemen and attentive lover. We will merely mention to friends about how you are the best sexual partner we have ever had without specifying any details. We will ensure this information gets back to you so that you are pleased by this but also delighted that we have been discrete. In turn we anticipate that you will be similarly complimentary about us and this provides us with fuel. We also like to ensure that the discarded individual learns of how we now have a sexual nirvana with you for reasons of gaining more fuel. Our gentlemanly conduct in this regard causes you to feel even more attracted to us and binds you closer to us. It also means we are setting you up for the inevitable fall also. We will drop subtle hints and cryptic clue about the healthy and vibrant state of our sex life by posting comments on social media such as:-

"Really tired today, somebody kept me up all night."
"Going for a quick nap. I will need my strength for tonight."
"Pass the energy drink, someone is coming round shortly."

We delight in letting other people know that we are enjoying a vibrant and healthy sexual relationship.

## Learning About Your Sexual Past

This is an absolute must for us. We thrive on information about you and that is no different in terms of gaining information about your past sexual exploits. We want to know how many partners you have had, the type of things you did with them in bed, whether you have engaged in a same sex scenario, whether you have engaged in group sex, the things you find distasteful and so on. This will all be done in a subtle and indirect fashion so as not to alarm you. We will present it as showing an interest in you. If we learn about any sexual abuse you have endured we will exhibit our learned sympathy and promise that we will make sure you are always respected and cared for whilst filing away this information about what has happened to you in the past for later use. Should you express any anxieties about sex we will use this as an opportunity to assuage those concerns causing you to be drawn closer to us by reason of our caring approach whilst noting this for future use? We will make reference to certain sexual activities and scenarios in books and on television, in film or in the media and use this as a means of drawing information from you. We are very good at remembering what you have told us, at storing this information away so we can rely on it later on. This will be used during the seduction phase to your benefit (and of course ultimately mine through the provision of fuel) to give you what you want as we mirror your sexual desires and to protect you from those things which may have hurt you in the past. All of this makes us a more attractive proposition. None of this questioning will be direct. There is no need for us to do this because you will provide this information willingly through the subtle and insidious application of our questioning. Much of it will be framed within compliments and flattery. We need this information as it must be used by us to further of our aim of controlling you and extracting fuel from you.

One of my former girlfriends was called Sam. She was, amongst other things, a very keen gardener. I learned about this hobby of hers from viewing various posts on her Facebook profile and noting that she belonged to certain horticultural groups as well. This allowed me to ask about gardening in the early stages of our relationship and it was a topic she enjoyed talking about. She would talk with enthusiasm about her own garden and would explain the work involved in it and what her favourite plants were. She was also a volunteer with the Royal Horticultural Society and would help out at shows. During our golden period I attended a few shows with her. In these early stages as I got to learn all about her love of horticulture I asked where her love of gardening came from. She was evasive in her answer and opted to change the subject. Naturally this did not pass me by and I realised that there was something that caused her concern in answering this. When we next attended a show I waited until we saw some children taking an interest in the butterflies in a glass house at these particular gardens.

"I should imagine you are pleased to see children getting involved in coming to the gardens?" I remarked and indicated towards the small group of young children.

"Yes, always need new blood coming into the society."

"I would not have though that gardening was something that children would really be into, not these days with so many electronic distractions."

"That's true; it is harder to get them to become interested, not like it was when I was younger."

"I daresay, how old were you when you got into gardening?"

"I was about six or seven I think."

"Pretty young then, was that through your dad?" I asked probing.

"No his brother, my uncle."

"Which one is he again?"

"George, his younger brother. Oh look at this butterfly HG," she remarked moving towards a clump of lupine flowers which had attracted several butterflies all of the same variety. She darted forward and I noted she had wanted to end that particular discussion.

    I kept this information about her early entry into gardening in my mind and also her reticence to discuss it in any detail. I would casually direct the conversation in that direction at an appropriate time as I began to gather little snippets of information. I learned that when she was younger she spent most Saturdays with her Uncle George which enabled her parents to have a day together. Her childhood home was in an apartment, an elegant one at that but with no access to a garden so it was deemed a "good thing" that she got out in the fresh air with Uncle George. He had an expansive garden but was somewhat precious about allowing Sam to touch his work. He did agree however to take her to some allotments and gained her a plot. I had no idea that there was such a waiting list for an allotment plot and the fact he had secured a plot for her (by persuading the Church of England who owned the allotment to allocate her a plot) was regarded as something of a coup. This was where she began to hone her skills all under the watchful eye of Uncle George. It took some time extracting this information from her as she was always reluctant to talk about it, preferring to move the conversation on to something else. I knew there was something wrong and realised it was to do with Uncle George. I gently chipped away and ascertained the location of her childhood plot. One day I engineered a situation whereby we pulled up next to the allotments and I began an attempt to cajole her into some sexual activity with me. She had shown no reluctance to do so in the past and had a healthy appetite for making love in the outdoors. She showed no such enthusiasm as I kept pointing out that there was a spot just over the fence where we could have sex. I pointed out that it was some kind of allotment and surely she would enjoy getting down to it amongst nature. She was reluctant and resisted my overtures but I kept going until she became really upset. I immediately apologised saying I had not realised she would become as upset as she had always enjoyed al fresco love making in the past.

"No, no, it is not your fault, it's just I can't, not here. This is my old allotment you see," she explained through her tears.

"Is it? I didn't know that. Why so upset then Sam, wouldn't it be extra special to make love in such a memorable location?" I pressed.

"No, no, I can't."

"Why not?"

"I just can't please, can we go?"

"Sure but I feel bad, I have upset you, let me help. What is it about here that is so bad?"

"Please I do not want to talk about it."

"Hey, it's okay, you can tell me anything, I won't think any less of you you know."

"I know you won't you aren't the judging type, it is just too upsetting."

"I want to help you; does this place bring back a bad memory or something?"

She nodded. I would not start the car and drive away. Under the auspices of caring about her well-being I kept pressing away until I finally got to the bottom of her distress. When she was a young girl her Uncle George allowed his allotment pal, a tall man she only knew as Skinner, to abuse her in one of the sheds. She was told she owed Uncle George for getting the plot and if she told anyone about what Skinner did then diesel fuel would be poured over her plot. Not only would this destroy her plants it would render the soil toxic thereafter. I of course offered suitable noises and gestures by way of my learned caring as we drove away and I had gathered a monumental segment from Sam's sexual past to use to my advantage. During the seduction stage I did this in a caring manner, ensuring that nothing was done to remind her of this trauma that she had suffered. She was thankful for this and her gratitude for my sympathetic manner (all manufactured of course) gave me fuel and also bound her tighter to me. I also had it waiting to use against her in the future. This past sexual occurrence provided me with a weapon to use both in the seduction and devaluation stages to assist me.

You may be surprised at just how often there are similar tales from those that I ensnare when I delve into their sexual past. From childhood abuse to teenage experimentation which went too far. From a sluttish period, through to hang-ups about sex brought about by a domineering mother, to disappoint sexual encounters. Inability to orgasm, dislike of oral sex, the need to be spanked, incest, trauma from being flashed at on a bus, issues revolving around toileting and sex, I have come across so many vulnerabilities. More than any other area of someone's life, more than money, career, family, children, and friends and so on, do the arena of sex result in people carrying some kind of baggage. I think this stems from the heightened and unrealistic expectations many people have of intimacy and sex, through to the way that some people use it as a weapon or a method of control, or just down to sheer incompetence. Very few of my victims have not had some kind of sexual sob story to relate to me. Many are fairly minor in nature but there are those which are substantial and allow me a bridge to that event by exploiting what has happened. This of course is something I shall deal with in the devaluation stage. What this means however is that for the benefits it reaps in both the seduction and the devaluation stages, the gathering of information about you sexual past is paramount.

## **Contraception**

The issue of contraception arises soon in the seductive stage as we are always keen to get you into bed. The question of contraception has us divided into the two camps. There is no grey hinterland here. There are those of us who have no interest at all in having children. We regard the arrival of children as a threat to the attention that we will receive. You, as mother, will dote on them and therefore no longer give us the attention we are entitled to and demand. Siblings and parents will be keen to focus their attention on the new arrival rather than us. This is a ghastly situation and one that cannot be tolerated. In order to avoid this scenario arising we will be keen to ensure that you are using contraception. We rarely choose to do this ourselves because we do not believe the responsibility should rest with us. It is your responsibility. If something goes wrong of course then we are able to blame you. We do not want children and therefore we will use other methods of binding you to us such as moving in, engagement and marriage.

The other side of this coin are those of us who want you to fall pregnant (or in the female variety of our kind wish to be made pregnant) at the earliest opportunity. This is done because we regard the existence of a child as the ultimate means by which we can bind you to us. Of course it is unilateral. You are expected to be dedicated to us by reason of this child whilst we can just up sticks and vanish without any sense of guilt or responsibility. We will use moving in, engagement and marriage as methods to bind you as well but often there is an initial expense associated with this whereas falling pregnant costs nothing. Of course there is a cost later but who knows where we might be by that stage, all that matters at the outset is that you are carrying our child (or we are carrying yours) and this will bind you to us. In this instance we will not use contraception, lie that we have or sabotage the contraception as well in order to maximise the prospects of conception.

**<u>The Orgasm</u>**

During the seduction phase your orgasm is most important to us. We want to deliver a delicious, earth-shattering, thigh-trembling orgasm which as you crying out your appreciation of us. As those endorphins course through you, we are establishing a further connection and creating your addiction to us. Naturally, the appreciation and admiration you exhibit as a consequence of the orgasm that we deliver to you gives us fuel. Accordingly, ensuring that you experience an orgasm is important. We like to deliver one every time and wherever possible more than one in each sex session with you. We want you conditioned to expect this when you couple with us so, as with so many other things, we can use this against you at a later stage.

By contrast our orgasm is not at all important to us. Yes if we have one it feels pleasant because that is the nature of one. Most men are driven to achieve orgasm by reason of biological programming to achieve procreation. Many women can enjoy sex irrespective of whether they have an orgasm, but with men, it is much more goal orientated. This is not the case with us. We are much more interested in the provision of fuel. We experience (or fake them – yes I have done this when inside someone) an orgasm and make a great performance from it. We salute how magnificent your technique is during this seduction stage in order to make you feel good so you will tell us how wonderful it is being with us. The result is more fuel and you drawing closer to us. By praising how good you are in bed and how our orgasms are mind-blowing, accompanied by such noises and much spasming and flailing off limbs then you feel even more connected to us. Look at the effect you have on us. You are amazing and this must mean that you are the one for us. Naturally nobody has made us come like this before and we will tell you this to reinforce the illusion that this perfect match .The reality is that we do not especially whether someone is good at sex in the way that you do. We know what you regard as great sex because we have studied it and we deliver it. Similarly we know exactly the things to say to you about how you make us feel, "By god you make my balls fizz", "I never thought it was going to stop washing over me", "I lost my sight for a moment there". These and other flattering comments will be made to support the fact that we have just experienced an almighty orgasm. In actual fact we often struggle to attain orgasm because we are so focused on giving you what we want that we forget about ourselves. Yes, the friction you apply by whatever bodily part you are using on us may well cause us to reach a climax but we do little to help you in that regard. We are not savouring the sensations as you might do, ensuring that body and mind work together to achieve orgasm. Our mind is elsewhere. It is working out what to do next to you and also thinking about the fuel you are currently providing and contemplating what further fuel can be obtained not only from you but others, often shortly after we have been lying with you. This means that our orgasm can be difficult to obtain and how some of you complain about the fact that we actually go on for too long. In the seduction phase when orgasm is difficult to obtain we will either:-

- Fake it if this feasible
- Brush the matter of by returning the focus on your pleasure and saying you can deal with me later

This creates an impression that not only are we formidable lovers with remarkable staying power and control but that we are more interested in your pleasure than our own. This will of course delight you. The situation is different in the devaluation scenario. Where we do orgasm we will exaggerate the effect with plenty bed-slapping, wall-punching and vocal tributes to you. Look at the effect that you have on us. You really know how to turn us on and deliver the goods; nobody has done this as well as you. Cue the various hyperbole all designed to make you feel good and draw you closer to us.

## The Sex Drive

In the seduction phase we exhibit an apparently voracious sexual appetite. We cannot get enough of it. We talk about it, promise you it, discuss what we are going to do to you and get on with it repeatedly. You will not have known a sex drive like the one that the narcissist shows. What you are actually witnessing is our voracious appetite for fuel. We just happen to be using sex to obtain it. There are three matters which arise from our high sex drive. The first is that we want to do it often to make you feel wanted and so you draw closer to us. The second is by giving you plenty of sex we cause you to comment favourably about us and therefore you provide us with fuel. The third is that we are natural performers and the sexual arena gives us the chance to show off and underline just how special we are. This high sex drive enables us to pester you (but in the most flattering way possible) for sexual contact in some form or other. In your mind we cannot get enough of you because you are so attractive to us, we love you so much and we are completely besotted with you. The sex is vigorous, exciting, tender and passionate. All of this of course is a façade as we put on a different mask according to which type of lover we decide to be, based on what you are seeking from our sexual coupling. Since the effects of sex have an especially potent effect on you and for us we naturally want to do it often. This presents as a very high sex drive. It is not the sex we are interested in. This just happens to be a useful way of getting fuel out of you. If singing was the most effective way we would be serenading you all day and night. Once again by creating this very high sex drive we are also generating something that can be taken away from you during the devaluation stage.

**Tenderness**

We know there are times when you want an energetic and vigorous sex session. Coming out of nowhere and taking you by surprise, some rough but not overly rough sex delights you. During this seduction stage however it is the tender, passionate love-making that you crave. We know this because we are fully familiar with the way you have been conditioned to regard sex, love and passion. We know this from our subtle questioning of you and our learning about what you want from sex in the early stages of our dance with you. Imagine that we have been able to read every book, every magazine and every newspaper that has something written about love and sex. Imagine that we have watched every film, documentary and television programme about the same subject. We have distilled it down to the key proponents and applied them to what we do. This will result in us knowing that a tender, loving manner when taking you to bed (not all the time, but much of the time) is truly the key to seducing you. We will arouse and stimulate you, that is a given, but we will layer onto this the long, lingering looks, the slow movement, the deep kisses and the words, especially the words. As master wordsmiths we will deliver line after line which has been copied from everything that we have been able to observe so far. We will construct a programme, like a computer, which we will roll out each time we know that it is necessary to show tender love. We will do this with all of our conquests saying the same things to the last one as you and the same things to the one after you. Yes, there will be some variations on a theme but the manner and approach is all the same. You are conditioned to expect tenderness and romance and we will deliver it in spadefuls. We do not mean any of it. It is purely a device to topple any resistance you may have, make you want us all the more and ensure you gush with fuel for us. By demonstrating a tender approach towards you when we engage in sex we are fulfilling your ideals and continuing to construct a false reality for you to occupy even though you have no idea that this is happening.

## New Sex Acts

In this seduction stage we will encourage you to engage in new sex acts which you will not have undertaken previously. The reason we do this is that we regard vanilla sex as ordinary and is for people who are of a lesser stature than us. We have to be different because we are special. In order to reinforce our elevated status we apply this to the sexual arena. We want you to try new and different things in between the sheets. During the seduction phase we do not do this by force or by unpleasantness. This will not sit with the charming and gentlemanly façade that we project. We will achieve your consent to engage in these new sexual methods through our salami-slicing approach, gently pushing the boundaries of your sexual tastes to cause you to indulge in new and novel experiences. There are several reasons as to why we want this to happen:-

- Fuel
- Exerting subtle control over you through the sexual arena
- Getting you to like certain practices which we can later withdraw
- Involving you in certain practices which may not be regarded as 'normal' which will allow us to hold your participation in these over you at a later date. We will have been careful not to engage in the behaviour ourselves or if we have we will deny we ever did it. You however are more than likely to have been filmed or photographed.
- This reinforces our special status

During this seduction stage where these boundaries will end up is very much up to you. We will push them albeit it gently. It may simply be getting you to try our different positions or mild bondage. In other instances there may be a greater indulgence in activities that fall within the BDSM remit or watersports for example. If we see that you will find the activity abhorrent we will not force the issue. We do not want to do anything (at least in this stage) to harm the positive fuel you provide us nor damage the façade that we are projecting towards you of our loving and decent self. The availability of so many different sexual practices and preferences allows us a massive choice. We do it to avoid the dull, vanilla sex and the connotations that come with that. We do it so you feel excited, that you are going on a sexual journey sailing to new horizons and engaging in something you have never done with the men you were once involved in. They are of course lesser men compared to us. We are causing you to have a sexual awakening and it is all done with your consent in a safe and loving environment. You experience new sensations and feel empowered as a consequence. We have allowed this to happen for you and you therefore provide us with your gratitude and admiration. You feel close to us because you have not done these things before. Some of them you might once have regarded as 'dirty' or 'deviant' but you have come to realise that when undertaken with the right person, someone who cares about you and loves you then you find that they are enjoyable, satisfying and invigorating. Much later you will look back on these times with us and remember with a bittersweet sensation how we opened you up to new experiences and new worlds and you thank us for it. You felt safe with us and the trust you placed in us when we did these things to you and with you showed just how much you loved us. In turn it showed us just how much fuel you had to provide to us. Of course, things took a darker turn but we are not quite ready for that.

Accordingly, throughout the seduction stage we use sex to achieve many aims. We make you fall for us, we make you feel bonded to us and close, we heighten your addiction to us and we exert control and manipulation. As usual, most of all we obtain fuel from you. It is worth now considering how it is that we create the addiction to us and our sexual proficiency.

# Why Are You Addicted To Our Sex?

I mentioned earlier in this book that one of the often heard laments about me and my kind is that our victims miss the sex. In addressing the question of why you are addicted to the sex we provided you with, there are two essential elements. The first is for what reason did we cause you to become addicted to the sexual experience with us. The second element is how did this happen?

We caused your addiction because as with everything we do it served our purposes. None of this is about you. It is about us. Everything has to be about us. We wanted you to become addicted to the sexual experience with us because then you would provide us with fuel. By finding us so exhilarating between the sheets you wanted sex with us often. This made us feel powerful because it enabled us to receive frequent bursts of quality fuel. We created a situation whereby you wanted to bed us, you wanted that sexual experience with us and that feeds our need for fuel and power. We brought about your addiction because as with any addict reasoning and logic becomes at best foggy and at worst absent. Consider the crack addict who wants his next hit. If he has no income other than state assistance he will rather go hungry, lose his electricity supply and not pay his rent in order to purchase his drugs. He will steal and not give a damn about the consequences to his victims or himself just so he can get enough money together to pay his dealer. He considers everything else minutiae compared to the need to get the money to buy his gear. When we cause you to be addicted you no longer act in a reasoned way. You put logic to one side in order to get your hit. This addiction means that you relinquish control over yourself and hand it to us instead. We dangle the keys to sexual nirvana in front of you. Certainly during the seduction stage we allow you repeated access and the only price we charge you is in fuel. You can provide this without difficulty and therefore you will engage in this sexual union repeatedly. What you do not realise is that you are becoming steadily addicted. This means you are actually racking up the charges that will be delivered to you at a later stage. You will be allowing yourself to be manipulated. You are eroding your free will and self-esteem. You are allowing yourself to be subjugated and dominated. All of this does not matter when you are in the seduction stage because we make it feel wonderful. When we present you with the bill and payment is required so begins the devaluation. You want more of this sex but you now need to pay. Not only have you racked up considerable credit but you are incurring further charges in your desperation to have sex with us. This shifts the balance of control firmly in our direction. Whereas once we gently coerced and pleasantly directed we are able to do as we please because you crave our sexual union so much. We make you addicted to give us power over you.

This also applies to the creation of something so that when we remove it, it hurts you deeply. There is a yawning chasm and you must fill it. You want us between the sheets once again, moving inside you and delivering that sexual hit that you want so much and which you became so used to. You want it so much that you will do nearly anything to get it and we know this. We know this and we will exploit it.

We not only made you addicted to provide us with fuel during the seduction stage but we did it so that you would keep on providing us with fuel during the devaluation. If sex did not matter to you, then you would cease to want it and a key method of extracting fuel from you would be lost. That is why we cannot just deliver to you satisfactory sex, we have to give you the best. Naturally this fits with our inflated opinions of ourselves as sexual masters of the universe but it is also necessary to bring about this addiction. Your drug cannot be cut with all manner of rubbish and thus its efficacy is reduced. You need the high quality, premium variety.

Accordingly, the reasons we make you addicted to your sexual experiences with us are as follows:-

- Fuel during seduction
- Fuel during devaluation
- Control

How did you become addicted to sex with us? Firstly, it is the best you have ever had and I have explained above why this is the case through our studied application of sexual techniques following observation and careful consideration of your preferences and reactions. Secondly, we provided it to you often. The more we gave you the more you wanted. Just like any drug. Thirdly, we may have ascertained a sexual vulnerability from your past and used our seduction of you to patch over this wound. We do not heal it because we are not healers and furthermore we will want to rip the wound open again later and pour salt into it. Fourthly and this is the major reason why you become addicted to the sex you had with us, it is because you always link it to love. We do dissuade you from making such a link. In fact we positively encourage you to do this. The way that we seduce you and the way that we love bomb you is designed to inject love into sex so that they effectively become indistinguishable from one another. We are fully aware that irrespective of how self-sufficient you may like to think that you are, how independently you might lead your life, you still have that desire for the white knight. Again, this relates to the way that you have been conditioned by society to regard love and romance. We know about this and exploit this. An honest examination of your thoughts and feelings will result in your admitting that at least on one occasion you have wanted that dashing knight to come riding in on his charger, sweep you in his arms and then take you through to the bedroom where he makes tender and delicious love to you. You have been conditioned to expect to be treated like a princess and we do this when we place you on that pedestal during our love bombing of you. Sex is no different. You want to be taken care of in the bedroom, loved and made to feel special. By providing all of this when we have sex with you then we are blurring the lines between sex and love, binding the two together. Since we are so magnificent in our delivery of delicious and rewarding sex then this entwined sex and love causes you to feel a very special kind of love, better than anything else you have experienced before. We apply all of the loving techniques when we have sex with you. The tender, romantic, slow and caring way we caress and hold you before easing into you all accords with this almost dream-like perception of how sex should be. We do however go further than this traditional model of the handsome prince making sweet, delicate love to his beautiful princess. When we suddenly take you from behind, hitch up your skirt and bend you over a worktop or the back of the settee and have vigorous sex with you we will look to ensure that this type of sex is entwined with love. How do we do this? With words of course. Words come easily to us and are cheap to use. So as we are hammering away and you are admittedly enjoying this spontaneous and energetic sex we will be telling you things such as:-

"I just had to have you. You were stood there and I was overwhelmed with love for you."
"I love you so much I needed to have you there and then."
"You do something to me that makes me almost lose control. That is how much I love you."
"I am so in love with you I just needed to be inside you."
"You make me crazy in love, I cannot help myself."

We reinforce this urgent sex with being linked to just how powerful and amazing our love is. The sex itself feels fantastic and when you hear those magical words being said to you from behind the two are melded together. The sex could not be regarded as romantic but that does not matter. Such rampant desire for you to be taken in this manner can only be a symptom of our love for you. This reinforcement will happen over and over again. From the obvious slow, tender love-making through to the quick knee-trembler on a table through to you fellating us in a parked car, we will cause you to associate all of these sexual acts as being manifestations of our truly remarkable love. Eventually, the word sex becomes eroded and every time we do something which is sexual in nature it is seen as love. Everything we do together in the sexual arena is born of love, is because of love and is a manifestation of love.

You are unable to resist this blurring of the boundaries between love and sex. You are not able to prevent sex actually subsuming the notion of love and cloaking itself in the name of love. This lack of resistance happens for two reasons. Firstly, the nature of our sexual couplings with you is so intense and enjoyable you want them and you want them repeatedly. Secondly, aside from the use of sex as a weapon, during the seduction stage you are being love bombed on lots of different fronts. We are saying beautiful things to you, writing you poems and love letters, buying you gifts, taking you to special places, looking after you when you feel ill, introducing you to our friends and so on. This onslaught of loving behaviour magnifies what we are doing on the sexual side. You are surrounded by loving behaviour so that it permeates into everything that we do with you, including sex. Accordingly, over time sex and love become bound up together. The great sex we provide to you translates as the marvellous love that we have for you. Sex is love, love is sex and it feels amazing causing you to become addicted to the sensation. We create lovesex and it is a powerful way of creating an addiction in you.

The status of our victims also plays a part in creating this addiction. We like to find people who are susceptible to addictive behaviour and in especially in the context of love and relationships. Our aim is to have all our targets become addicted to this lovesex and through the powerful campaign of love bombing, using sex as a weapons and all the other manipulative techniques we apply, this will happen. There are however certain types of victim who are far more susceptible to becoming addicted to this lovesex and this makes matters easier for us. There are, in essence, three categories of victim who are prone to being addicted more easily than a 'standard' victim.

## **The Crush Victim**

If during our early conversations and exchanges we ascertain that you referred to having crushes on boys (but you did not have boyfriends) and on for example pop and film stars then this will flag with us that you will be more susceptible to becoming addicted to our lovesex. This adoration and idealisation of people who are unobtainable signifies to us that given access to somebody special, namely us, will result in you feeling special and that childhood crush you had on Tony Hadley from Spandau Ballet is transferred to us. I have written on several occasions about how returning you to childhood is a powerful method of control. This is in this vein. We recognise how you felt about that film star and how you experienced a dizzying euphoria every time you thought about them saw them on the screen or looked at their picture on that poster over your bed. You dreamt up fantasies about you and that person and this became etched on your psyche. Someone who would watch a boy at school from afar, write love letters to that boy but never send them and who would again dream about a life together is someone who regularly experienced crushes. You generated an intoxicating euphoria, albeit manufactured on a fallacy, about this particular person. Imagine how powerful the effect will be when you actually are able to be with someone brilliant, kind, wonderful and attentive? This will shunt you straight into the realms of addiction. You never achieved the outcome you desired of being on the arm of that special person. We will now give you that and by knowing you once had crushes on people we know that you are particularly susceptible to becoming addicted to our lovesex and naturally we will use this to our advantage.

**The Fix Addict**

The desire to fix and heal is the hallmark of the empath and is one of the reasons when we commence our devaluation of you that you cling to us. You want to fix us. You want to mend the relationship so that it returns to the golden period once again. You had it once so why can it not be attained a second time? Your innate need to help, fix and heal is a laudable trait in you. It is something we want from our victims in order to ensure they keep hanging on as we extract the negative fuel from you. It also tells us that you are somebody who will be susceptible to addiction to our lovesex. The reason for this is that you will think that just another conversation will make things all right again. Just another evening together doing something pleasant. Just another passionate night in bed together. Just one more. Like the alcoholic or drug addict you keep telling yourself that just one more drink or one more line of cocaine and everything will be alright. You convince yourself, despite all evidence to the contrary, that another 'hit' with me will fix things. You sense that a corner is just about to be turned, that redemption is but a conversation away and this is why you keep hanging on in there. Somebody who thinks like this because they want to make everything all right and will keep going in the hope this will happen even though everything else points against this, is someone who will readily become addicted to our lovesex.

These people have a predisposition to addiction because they can never give up something. Our lovesex has the same effect.

## **The Broken Addict**

I have mentioned in other works how we do like to find people who are damaged. It may be the case that they have been tenderised by one of our kind previously which makes them easier prey for us. It may be that they are so desperate to expunge the horrific experience of their previous relationship they miss all the red flags and warning klaxons. In terms of their susceptibility to addiction, the Broken Addict ranks highly. You have experienced considerable pain from a failed relationship before we came along. It does not necessarily have to have been at the hands of one of kind. It may be an intimate relationship, a familial one or a working relationship. What matters is that you are in pain. Just like the person who drinks too much, takes recreational drugs too often, over-eats or gambles all of these actions, when performed too often become addictions. All of these actions are carried out by these people in order to do one thing; blot out the pain. The usual addictions are used as crutch to help people deal with the pain they are suffering. They are trying to fill a hole. They choose those subjects who provide a quick fix and make everything seem alright for a short time before the crashing low begins and they must return to their chosen fix time and time again and of course in greater and greater quantities. Their chosen fix will be damaging them but their sense of reason has been pushed off balance. Their health, work, finances and relationships all suffer because of this reliance on a particular fix. This is the terrible outcome for those who are in pain and become addicted in order to try and fix that pain.

    We do exactly the same. We do not come with drugs or alcohol but our lovesex. The pain you experience arising from that broken relationship is dulled and removed by you being allowed access to our lovesex. You feel good again and you come to rely on our lovesex as a means of keeping that pain at bay. What is worse with this addiction, than say one to gambling or drugs, is that we know you are in pain. The drug dealer will not. We know exactly what has caused the awful pain which tears through you and we present our lovesex as the panacea to cure all those ills in the full knowledge that you will grasp it with both hands and in turn become addicted to it.

Accordingly, you are addicted to sex with us and the glorious sensations that it creates because of:-

- How good it is in itself
- How frequently we provide it to you
- The backdrop of love bombing that it comes with and is associated with
- Your vulnerability
- The creation of lovesex
- Your susceptibility to addiction

Like any addict when you are denied that which you are addicted to you will suffer consequences. You will do practically anything to get it back again and in the hands of people like us you are in a dangerous place. This leads us on to the topic of how sex is used during devaluation.

# Sex in the Devaluation Stage

There comes a point in your relationship with our kind when we knock you off that pedestal and send you sprawling into a quagmire of misery, dejection and confusion. Every so often we will reach a hand out to you, the golden period blazing behind us as we lift you out of the nightmare only to then deposit you straight back into it after a short interval. We pull you out and then push you back in over and over again until we eventually cast you to one side. It is a disorientating, confusing and bewildering time which makes no sense at all to you. You cannot fathom out why someone who loves you and loves you so perfectly can do this to you. It does not add up. It is not logical. You go round and round in circles trying to work out why this has happened, what could you have done to deserve this horrendous treatment and how does it just happen in an instant? You will debate scenarios with your friends and family who are all equally helpless as they have no idea who you are dealing with. You will try and talk to us about this sudden change but get nowhere. We know full well what we are doing but we will deny it, we will blame you by telling you that you are making things up and imagining what is happening. We will blame you for making us behave like this. Any attempt to gain understanding or resolution from us will never be achieved. You will not be able to think straight because we have applied so many manipulative tools against you. You were deliriously happy on Friday evening and by Saturday afternoon you are upset, confused and bewildered. You will try so hard to make things right, after all, they were brilliant once so surely that can be achieved again can't it? You want to fix things; you want everything to be alright, it is central to your nature to want to understand what has gone wrong and to make it right. Add to all of this the fact that we have caused you to become addicted and reliant on us, you will find yourself in a terrible position. This confusion and reliance means that we have you in a place where we can effectively do as we please. You are vulnerable and now about to suffer the consequences of being subjected to a sustained campaign of devaluation.

Why does this happen? In short it is because of fuel. We need fuel. You provided it through positive fuel during the golden seduction period. You then do not provide it as often, in the quantity we need or of the quality we require. We will be obtaining fuel from other sources but in order to remedy this deficiency and also to punish you for letting us down we commence our devaluation of us. There is nothing you can do to prevent it happening other than escaping us but this does not happen. Why? Because you have become addicted to us for the reasons I explained in the previous chapter and key to that addiction is how we used sex during our seduction. This was fundamental in creating the addiction and is a large part of your addiction. We will occasionally offer you respite during the devaluation and everything seems wonderful for a short period. Your relief at this return to the golden period once again provides us with further fuel. You also feel vindicated because you have proven that you can get back to the golden period. It is merely a ruse. It is a temporary state of affairs when we resurrect the illusion in order to keep you with us. We will shatter it again after a period of time and continue with the devaluation. This will cause you to churn out negative fuel once again but you will not give up. You got the golden period back once so guess what? Yes you will keep trying even though we are actually pushing you deeper and deeper into the quagmire, demolishing your confidence, shattering your self-esteem, making you anxious, belittling you, assaulting you, ruining your finances and isolating you. You are exhausted, unable to cope, disorientated and cling in desperation to us thinking we are the life raft that can save you when in actual fact we are the very instrument which is making matters worse for you. This is how insidious and dangerous we are.

Thus having established that devaluation will happen and a brief explanation as to why this is, what is the role of sex in this devaluation. In a similar vein to its use during seduction, it is all about gathering fuel from you (although this time of a negative variety) and controlling you. During devaluation sex will primarily be used in two ways:-

- It is removed because we regard you as sexless; and
- When we do engage in it is used as a tool to devalue you

When you have failed in your obligation to provide us with fuel and devaluation starts, your sexual attraction which was a means of gathering positive fuel also wanes. We begin to regard you as sexless. In certain situations this means that sex is completely withdrawn (see below) and sexual engagement occurs with other people. This is in effect a manifestation of the Madonna/whore complex which I will address later. In other situations there will be a withdrawal of sex but not totally as the sexual arena will be used purely for the purpose of devaluation because the negative fuel to be gathered is so enticing. The Victim Variety of narcissist is most likely to withdraw sex altogether owing to his stance as being largely uninterested in it but also because the attraction of his primary care giver as the Madonna appeals to him particularly. The cerebral narcissist will shift the emphasis by engaging in verbally humiliating sexual behaviour in order to gather fuel, whilst largely abstaining from the physical act. Somatic and elite narcissists are less prone to complete withdrawal as they see the sexual act as still available to them for the purposes of gathering fuel through devaluation.

The use of sex during the devaluation stage is a dark place where the most intimate act is used against you repeatedly. Let us examine the many ways it is used during this stage.

## Withdrawal

This is one of the major uses or more accurately, non-uses of sex during the devaluation stage. In the golden period of seduction we gave you lots of wonderful, passionate sex. It is now time to take it away. How does this manifest?

- We no longer initiate sex
- When you try and initiate sex we reject you
- We deliberately talk about other women to raise the suggestion in your mind that we are having sex with them and not you
- We watch pornography (more on this later) in order to show we are interested in sex but just not with you
- We will turn our back on you in bed
- We will sleep in the spare room or on the sofa to be away from you and the usual arena of sex
- We will accuse you of being a nymphomaniac and not caring about feelings, the fact we are tired from working so hard to support you and the family etc.
- We will accuse you of having affairs to legitimise our withdrawal of sexual interest in you
- We will accuse you of dressing like a slut so that you do not appeal to us

The removal of sex in any relationship causes problems. The removal of sex in a relationship with us is devastating. Like much of what we do, we take you up high purely so that there is further for you to fall. Everything we do is designed to have this effect during the devaluation stage. We bought you beautiful gifts and now we buy you the wrong things or nothing at all. We took you to dine at expensive restaurants and now we never take you anywhere. Everything that was once wonderful is either removed or made awful. Sex is no exception.

Since we have caused you to bind love and sex together, the removal of our sexual interest in you hurts you. It upsets you and wounds you. It causes you to question us, pleading with us to explain why we will no longer sleep with you. Your reactions of bewilderment, upset, anger and distress all provide us the negative fuel that we want.

The prospect of the reinstatement of sexual relations with us also allows us to exert control over you. You will agree to do things that you would ordinarily would have resisted both within and without the sexual sphere. The ability to have such control over you, to manipulate how you react gives us our fuel and makes us feel powerful.

Do not think our withdrawal is because we have 'gone off' you or that we no longer find you attractive or a turn on. We never did to begin with. I understand that the noise we made, the gestures we exhibited and the things we said all seemed so convincing. Of course they were. That was deliberate. We made it seem like sex with you was the best thing in the world. I will remind you of the comments I made at the outset of this book. We derive some physical stimulation from engaging in sex acts with you but the reality is that we are just masturbating with your body parts. No matter how attractive or sexy you are, no matter how wanton, experienced and flexible you may be none of it matters because that is not what matters to us when we use sex in our seduction of you. Accordingly, you may try and lose weight, buy new clothes, change hairstyle, take up new interests and even have plastic surgery in order to make yourself more attractive to us and end the withdrawal. None of it will work. The only way you will make yourself more attractive to us is by giving us better grade fuel and since the negative fuel outweighs the positive fuel you are on a hiding to nothing. Withdrawal allows us to crash you into the ground so that you provide us with heightened emotional reactions and therefore more fuel.

There is more however to our withdrawal than just doing it to hurt and confuse you. We do it in order to preserve our sense of being special. You will be well-acquainted with our sense of self-importance and our belief that we are superior to all of those around us. In order to maintain this status we must act accordingly. One way of doing so is to withdraw from people and not just sexually. During the seduction stage we are all over you, we are everywhere and contacting you in every manner we can. You are blown away by this because this is part of the love bombing. When we begin our devaluation of you we regard this period of repeated exposure as amounting to over exposure and thus we believe this has reduced our currency. Familiarity can breed contempt. We blame you for causing us to do this. We blame you for causing us to engage in love bombing which has cheapened our worth by us appearing frequently. In the same way that a Z list celebrity becomes derided for turning up to the opening of an envelope, we regard this over exposure as a risk to our special status and it is you who is at fault for this. If you had not presented yourself to us so we had to try and lure you in, we would not have over exposed ourselves in this way. In order to ensure that our special status is not eroded further we withdraw from you. In the sexual sphere, we have provided you with copious amounts of sex. Now we wish to withdraw and we will do so. This will hurt you but it also enables us to retain our special status as a sexual god. This will allow us to retain a special sense of self as being wanted, lusted over and desired because of our elevated status beyond ordinary people.

Accordingly any attempt you may make to draw us back to engage in sex with you will be doomed. You are fighting against the fuel we draw from hurting you this way and our need to ensure the preservation of our special status. Any resumption of sex will be on our say so and in the manner we deem to be appropriate. This latter point leads us to commit acts which you would usually refuse to participate in as being unacceptable, but your level of desperation and the removal of your critical reasoning and defences means you will engage in such behaviour in the hope of securing the resumption of sex to feed your addiction once again.

## The Put Downs

Denigrating somebody in a sexual sense is a powerful means of drawing fuel and controlling them. Insulting somebody will usually draw a reaction from all but the most confident, self-absorbed and/or thick-skinned individuals. Insulting someone in a sexual sense is virtually impossible to ignore. During devaluation we will do this repeatedly. We will do such things as:-

- Ridicule your performance in bed by suggesting you are useless (despite the many compliments we will have showered you with previously, which only adds to your hurt and confusion)
- Denying we like something that we once proclaimed to love doing with you
- Triangulating you with past lovers by praising their sexual performances and telling you how she would do x and y better than you
- Triangulating you with a current lover by praising their sexual performances
- Calling you frigid despite there being evidence to the contrary
- Calling you sluttish and a nymphomaniac despite evidence to the contrary
- Labelling you as homosexual when you are not and vice versa
- Expressing our view that we are actually homosexual because sex with you has horrified us and left us scarred

- Mocking you by saying your breasts are too small or too large, that your vagina is too tight or slack or similar

These put downs will all be sexual in nature, will bear no resemblance to the reality in which you operate and are designed to hurt you and make you give us fuel. Putting you down reinforces our superiority. We also do it as a reaction to our disgust at coupling with someone as weak and inferior as you. Only yesterday we could have been declaring our undying love and how pert your bottom is and then today we will tell you we never loved you, you have trapped us and we hate your flabby backside. Your failure to give us the fuel we want and thus initiate the devaluation results in us realising that we have been duped (even though it is the other way around). You have trapped us in this relationship with this dud. How could someone as brilliant as us fall for this? How horrible you must be to do this to someone who has treated you so well. This is the twisted mindset that we adopt. This makes no sense to you and it does not because you are regarding it through your reality. It makes perfect sense in our reality. You have failed in your obligation. You are a fraud and a charlatan and for that you must be punished. Hence the put downs begin. This happens to give us fuel which of course is what it is really all about. The fact that these put downs can be framed in a sexual sense makes their bite and sting worse. The comments will be wounding and because they are of such an intimate and personal nature your response will be all the more heightened which is exactly what we want.

Something else that you ought to be aware of is that with the put downs they reveal just how misogynistic our kind really are. We are misogynists because in order to control and oppress you we have to have a deep-seated hatred of you. This drives our desire, along with the prospect of fuel, in order belittle and control you. This misogyny is hidden because our façade of wonderful pleasantness and charm makes us seem as if we adore and respect women. We do not. We hate the fact that we are shackled to you in order to draw fuel from you and therefore we hate you. Since most narcissists are men, this means that misogyny rises to the fore. This is evidenced in the use of sexual put downs. Consider the following words:-

Slut
Slag
Whore

What did you think of when you read those words? I should imagine you thought of a woman in some way. Those words are not linked with men are they? There is no true male equivalent of slut. There are words designed to insult men based on their gender, words such as sissy, pansy, wet or drip, but they are not as powerful as slut. We use these sexual putdowns to unmask our misogyny. We regard all women as untrustworthy, evil and out go get us. Snakes with tits.

Consider the following put downs which we will regularly use against you:-

> Gorgon
>
> Crone
>
> Frigid
>
> Slattern
>
> Harridan
>
> Tart
>
> Iceberg
>
> Tramp
>
> Hooker
>
> Prick teaser
>
> Jezebel
>
> Battleaxe
>
> Dyke
>
> Ballbuster
>
> Witch

I could go on but look at this list and see how many of these put downs appertain to something sexual. You are a prick-tease by flirting with us but not delivering the goods. Is there a male equivalent? A clit-teaser perhaps? Maybe, but it is hardly in general parlance is it? Jezebel is a

Biblical reference to a sexually manipulative woman. Tramp means a sluttish, promiscuous woman but apply it to a man and it means he is downtrodden and homeless. There is a cast array of words which are used against women (and not against men by way of an equivalent) and often used in a sexual sense. This may say more about the patriarchal nature of society and that is not something I propose to address here. What it does allow however is for us to select a vast array of sexual put-down labels for use against you. I have little doubt that as you read that list if you were called any of them you would feel hurt and angry by their use. We know that and that is why during devaluation we shower them around like confetti.

**Promiscuity**

We are promiscuous. This is because we want to obtain fuel from as many sources as we possibly can. We usually do not care where this attentive fuel is coming from (hence why a number of our kind will engage in same sex sexual acts because what matters is the attention not the gender or sexuality of the person behind that attention. The sexuality only has any relevance if this means a challenge as I have discussed above). If we need fuel and there is a method of gaining it through a sexual method it really is a case of any port in a storm. Promiscuity enables us to gather fuel from lots of different sources. Using sexuality to do this is the equivalent of us being like a child in a sweet shop. We have no concerns about sexual norms or how society regards someone like us who will flit from sexual partner to another at the drop of a pair of knickers. We are above such reproach and admonishment. We do not care if society frowns about the way we behave as we move from one person to another. We may be promiscuous during the seduction stage purely as a means of gaining fuel but we will keep this hidden from you. Instead, we will unveil our promiscuity and furthermore increase it during the devaluation process in order to gather more fuel and to lash out at you. Our kind is notoriously promiscuous and I recall when my promiscuity arose.

I remember the day, or more accurately that the floodgates were opened on my promiscuity. It was when I attended a particular university for the purposes of an admission interview. It was early December and orange and yellow lamps lighted up this historic and beautiful university city as a little mist clung to the narrow alleyways and courtyards. I had concluded my two interviews (read Fury if you want to know more about how they progressed and how one interview influenced me) and returned to the junior common room to meet up with two other candidates. They were applying to the same college but to read a different subject to me. They were both English literature students. He was from Greenock in Scotland and she was a bookbinder's daughter from Cambridge in England. Beer was consumed, stories swapped and the fellow from Greenock retired to his room. The bookbinder's daughter, she was called Sarah, came back to my room and we talked before we climbed into bed together. I had a girlfriend at the time and whilst there had been dalliances with other girls I had not slept with another. That changed that night. And in the morning too. Sarah wandered away across the quadrangle to her room and I rose from my bed to seek out the bathroom. She decided to stay another day at the college because she wanted to spend time with me. I was happy for her to do so as I waited around, as was customary, in case an interview arose at another college. The following day we both departed, she to the east and me to the west and once I alighted at the train station near to my girlfriend's house I went straight round to see her. She was pleased to see me and embraced me with enthusiasm. I returned the enthusiasm. I had no sense of guilt at my infidelity. Nothing at all. Instead, I revelled in the way I had taken Sarah to my bed and now strode into my then girlfriend's bedroom with her asking with admiration how my interview had progressed and what the college was like.

Following that first time, I never looked back. I cheated left, right and centre. With that girlfriend and with all subsequently. Why did I do it? Way back then I realised how good it made me feel but I had no understanding of why I actually did it. Something always drove me to do it. I realised that the relevant girlfriend would be upset if she knew what I had done but this never stopped me. I never gave it a second thought. Even as I was locked in an embrace with some relative stranger and an image of the girlfriend formed in my mind I felt no tug of conscience, remorse or guilt. All I knew was that I was able to seduce, pull, entice and ensnare everywhere I went. I would meet someone and always find something attractive about them - it might be the colour of their hair, the length of their legs, their accent, the way they rolled the letter r, the fact they drank with a straw or the size of their breasts. It might be their enthusiasm for a particular band, their recollections of travelling or the manicured nails. Each and every one had some kind of attraction. I could not resist trying to ensnare someone in order to bring him or her under my spell. It was then that I realised what it was that really drew me to them, it was the promise of their attention. I realised I was able to get them hooked on me. I had convinced myself that I was drawn to them for some other reason but it dawned on me that I was just telling myself that as a reason. A reason that I required to explain this compelling desire to couple with someone. However, that was not the real reason. The truth was that I wanted their attention on me and this was the way to get it.

Yes, it was pleasant engaging in that first kiss and I enjoyed the sensations that arose when the embrace escalated but it was not what I actually I wanted. I wanted them to praise me. I wanted them to become transfixed by me and for them to shine their spotlight firmly on me. The promiscuity has always continued and it does not matter who with it is the fact that I am able to do seduce and by so doing gather that starry-eyed admiration, those pleasing words and the attention. This engagement does not end with behaving in a promiscuous fashion. I will engage in discussions with a stranger of my own sex, at a bar, a railway platform or in a lift. I have no desire to seduce them sexually for that is not my preference but I do cause them to like me and in so doing give me that fuel that I need.

Often I feel like admitting my repeated transgressions straight away to the relevant girlfriend of the time but I have no desire to puncture my primary source of fuel by doing this. I do find it interesting how they always react with such alarm and distress on the odd occasion I do make such a confession. If I tell them how well I got on with a random male in an exchange at a bar, someone with whom I have swapped views, thoughts and opinions, I receive a smile and a comment of,

"Always good to make new friends."

Yet an admission of coupling with a stranger results in hysteria even though to me these interactions are similar. Yes, one might yield greater fuel than the other might but in terms of intimacy, they are equally redundant. That is not why I do it. I do not do it because I want to savour the sensation of another's mouth against me. I do it because I want them to give me fuel. I can understand how you may be aghast if in a normal relationship a partner behaves with infidelity but to our kind it just about the attention, the admiration, the fuel. You have such a great hang up because sex is involved. That is just the gateway device to me. If I could get the attention another way so that it provides such fuel then believe me I will do it. However, in your world, on the whole, the act of a sexual union accords a greater connection between two people, which means you yield more fuel and are more inclined to keep providing it as you seek more from the liaison.

Our promiscuity arises to enable us to achieve fuel. From the new target who is seduced by us and from you should we alert you in some way (either in whole or in part) to our new interest. The condemnation that is attached to promiscuity when in a relationship means that your reaction just provides us with even more fuel. There is a risk of your supply being punctured by this revelation but it is a calculated risk and is often done when the quality of your supply generally has started to wane.

To us promiscuity when in a relationship is merely a means to an end. To you, well, you behave as if it is the end of the world. It really is not as far as we are concerned.

## Infidelity

A cousin of promiscuity is infidelity. We will be unfaithful to you at some point. That is a guarantee. When we are first seducing, you we will be in the process of devaluing someone else leading to his or her discard. We most likely will have withdrawn sex from the victim who we are devaluing and be having sex with you as the new object of our seduction. This does not mean that since you are the apple of our eye we will be faithful to you. We will have intermittent sex with the person who is subjected to the devaluation either as a means of giving them a short golden period again or for the purposes of extracting further fuel by subjecting them to humiliating sexual activities. We will also be courting other prospects also as well as you and therefore there is a strong likelihood we will be bedding that person also. We will, when seducing you, maintain an image of fidelity since that is what you expect. If you are conducting an affair with us, we will assure you that our current partner (whom we are devaluing) never has sex with us, we sleep in separate beds and so on. We will bemoan the fact they never have sex with us in order to draw sympathy from you as the new prospect.

By contrast, we will triangulate you as the new prospect with our current partner. We will drop heavy hints that we are being unfaithful or even actively admit it in order to further the hurt. Our rationale behind this is that monogamy is for the little people and this does not include us. That would make us less special and we cannot have that. We are entitled to seek sex outside of a relationship because this is our inalienable right to enable us to obtain fuel. We feel no guilt in doing this, we do not respect any vows we may have given to remain faithful to you and we have no qualms about coupling with someone else. The reason for this is that we have to do it and in a perverse way, the only reflection on you is that you are not giving us the fuel we need. It is not a reaction to what you look like, what you do, who your friends are or what your interests might happen to be. We will of course use them, as a method of lashing out at you should you try and question us about our infidelity because as I have explained in **Manipulated** we will deploy blame shifting frequently when we are under attack. It is often the case that when a partner learns of the infidelity of their partner that they will scrutinise their own conduct.

"Is it something I have done?"

This means that you will examine your own behaviour and try to improve in some way because you will want to salvage our relationship. The fact of your addiction means you do not want to let us go. You will be mightily hurt and offended by our infidelity but you will try to find some way of fixing it because that is what you like to do. If our infidelity shows any risk of you departing, we will hastily reinstate the golden period, a mini-Hoover if you will, to stop you departing from us. Most of the time however, because of the way you are, you blame yourselves (often because we warp your way of thinking to do this) and you try to patch things over. Your need to resolve matters results in you clinging to us notwithstanding our fidelity. Indeed, in some instances you want to prove that you are better than the person we committed our infidelity with. You want to fight to retain us and ensure that our relationship triumphs.

We will also use infidelity as a means by which to control you and make you do what we want:-

"If you gave me more attention I would not go elsewhere."

"If you put out more often I would not have to get it from someone else."

"Perhaps if you hadn't let yourself slide I wouldn't stray would I?"

"If you thought more about me rather than yourself perhaps it would not have happened?"

"I won't leave you, I should, but I will stay but some things are going to have to change."

You are the victim. We have committed the transgression but other than when we fear you might leave us and sever our supply of fuel, we will not apologise but pin the blame on you. You will have been subjected to a succession of manipulation wiles in order to browbeat you and lower your resistance so that when we unveil our infidelity we use it as a method of getting what we want from you, namely more fuel and more control.

## Prostitutes

You may think why would a self-proclaimed sexual Olympian who can seduce anybody he wants and lure him or her into bed have any need to visit a prostitute? You may think that since a prostitute is offering sex in exchange for money then there is no conquest involved and therefore there is nothing to be gained by us. You may consider that we would find it an insult to our seductive qualities to have to pay for sex. You may also take the view that the prostitute is not going to provide us with the reactions we would normally receive and therefore there is little point in us using them. These are all valid observations but the fact is we do use prostitutes.

You will by now realise that it is nothing to do with the sex. It is not because we want to experience a different woman to the one(s) we have been having sex with regularly. It is not because this prostitute might be broadminded compared to the partner we are with (believe me when you are in the devaluation phase nothing is off limits in terms of getting you to do all manner of depraved and indecent acts). No, the reasons we use prostitutes are as follows:-

- They are a challenge.

- The provision of fuel

- The opportunity to use them to triangulate

- The reinforcement of our superiority

The sex with a prostitute is the same as sex with you is the same as when we masturbate. The sex is just a sideshow. The challenge arises in getting the prostitute to climax. A prostitute will provide you with the allotted hour or until you have climaxed and then it is adios. We are able to last for a considerable time and therefore we like to try to make the prostitute climax. This happens and when it does, it provides me with a rush of fuel as her reaction amounts to considerable admiration after overcoming the challenge. If she does not then that is a problem of hers and nothing to do with me.

We also engage in taking the services of a prostitute and then not pay them for it. You may be surprised at the number who will, after suitable charm, agree to provide their services for a down payment and the balance being paid afterwards. I need to go to a cashpoint so let us do that afterwards. Some may march you to a cashpoint beforehand but some will not and foolishly trust us. We will either not pay up or take back the cash we have had handed over, kick them out of the car or motel room and then we are on our way surging on the power of having caused and angry and frustrated reaction and we got something for nothing. It is not the fact that we got sex for free it is the fact that we duped them. In actual fact, we could sit with them for an hour, talk, and then not pay them. What matters is that they have lost out and their reaction to that provides us with fuel.

In the same way we use infidelity to triangulate we will do the same with our use of prostitutes. We know that you find the idea that we have been with a street girl or high-class escort something that is dirty and despicable. Your reaction to being told that we have done this or to finding evidence of our use of prostitutes gives us fuel. We really are not bothered about having sex with them; we just relish how you will react when you find out about them. During the act with a prostitute, we will be reflecting on how you will respond and react when you duly find out and this makes us feel powerful. Just by contemplating your reaction, we enjoy a surge of fuel. We will use prostitutes in our triangulation because they are easy to obtain as well. We use some money (most likely yours) and we have secured their services. It is not their services we are interested in them but the fact that we are able to obtain some evidence to wave under your nose (such as a flyer, browsing history on the internet or a suspicious credit card receipt) and thus triangulate with.

Our use of prostitutes also reinforces our superiority. In the way we regard ourselves as superior because we can charm anyone into bed, we are superior because our economic prowess can be used to buy intimate time with another human being. How worthless must this person be if they have to resort to doing this? We of course conveniently ignore what does that make us by using a prostitute. We can do that easily. We do not use them for sex because we can get that from anyone. We are not inferior because we choose to use them for our purposes. Once again, the end always justifies the means.

The same rationale applies to strippers and lap dancers. We like the attention they are providing to us. Yes, we are paying them to be like that but we know they are actually attracted to us, how could they not be. We like to string them along sitting chatting to the dancer for as long as possible as she provides us with compliments.

"Oh you work in IT/the law/finance/litter collection that is brilliant. You must find that so interesting?"

On and on they go praising and showing attention and interest in the hope of gaining some money for a dance and then when I head off to the bar instead I can see they are trying to smile through the disappointment of failing to secure a sale and that feeds me fuel. I may go back and carry on talking with her again; raising the hope inside her that this time, she will secure a dance with me. I string her along and then disappoint again. Sound familiar at all, the old push and pull. You are not the only ones who are subjected to this.

## Group Sex

During devaluation, you are expected to engage in this. Your resistance to our suggestions will be low and your desire to regain our sexual approval and congress will be substantial. Whereas during the seduction stage we subtly and pleasantly introduced new sex acts to you in a salami slicing fashion we can, during the devaluation stage introduce those things, which you may find degrading and unsavoury much more directly. It usually comes accompanied with comments such as these:-

"You love me don't you? Well if you do love me you will do it won't you?"

"Try it, just for me, I promise it will just be that once."

"How do you know you will not like it if you have not tried it?"

"If you want to stay with me you will do it."

"Is it any wonder I go elsewhere when you are this boring?"

"Do it or I will do x"

"(Former girlfriend) would do this and you said you love me more than she did, now is the time to prove it."

"Just do it for me and we can have the weekend away together."

"We need to do this if our relationship is to survive. I am trying to keep us together, don't you want that?"

I know there are plenty of people who engage in group sex. It may be a drunken threesome involving a friend or participation in swinging parties. One party is usually a little reluctant to go along with it but he or she has no major reservations and if they do not do it, the other person or persons involved tend not to make anything of it. This is not applicable in a situation involving our kind.

We want to involve you in group sex for a number of reasons. For instance, let us take at its most basic level a threesome involving one of your friends. We will initiate and make this happen because:

- We have the opportunity to show off our sexual prowess to two people and gain additional fuel from doing so

- We like to arrange people because we objectify them. We will spend part of the experience directing you and the other person. Your reactions to our direction will also provide us with fuel

- It underlines the control we have over you

- If you object and become upset this will provide us with fuel

- It may be something you are ashamed of doing so we can bring it up at a later stage and use it against you. We may do this by telling someone else whose views you respect that you indulged in such behaviour so it shames and upsets you. We may use it to accuse you of being too much into the other person and not enough into us in order to provoke a reaction from you.

- We are exhibitionists and group sex is another way of gaining admiration and adoration

We have no issue with watching you being taken by another man. We will want to discuss it with you afterwards and listen as you explain that he was nowhere near as good as us and that it made you remember just how good we are at sex. The power that we derive from having you do what we want and then offer up your praise of our sexual prowess feeds us fuel. We relish your initial objection at these suggestions your protests providing us with further fuel but we know that you will submit. It also underlines that you are inferior and the slut we always believed you to be because you engage in such behaviour. If you had any self-respect, you would not do this but you clearly have none. Any protests that you may issue about how we forced you to do it will later be dismissed. You wanted to do it because you are that way inclined. We know our stance is borne out of hypocrisy but it does not matter to us, so long as we are achieving our fuel and exerting our control over you.

## **The Orgasm**

In the seduction stage, the granting of an orgasm to you was the ultimate aim when we slid between the sheets with you. This has now altered. Whereas before we exhibited skill and proficiency in how we stimulated you, now we act with the clumsiness of a virgin and as if the female form is alien to us. On some occasions, we will do all the things we know that do not arouse you and none of the things that do resulting in you becoming frustrated. This gives us fuel. You may even apologise blaming yourself saying that you are tired or stressed and telling me it does not matter. I will feign disappointment and wonder aloud what I have done wrong in order to gain reassurance, sympathy and admiration from you. Should you dare to criticise my performance then this will ignite my fury and I will lash out at you shouting that the reason you were not aroused is down to you:-

"You are frigid that is the problem."

"You are sex-mad, I just want to cuddle."

"Your problem is that you want it too much, you expect too much of me, I am not a machine you know."

"You've been playing around with someone else that's why you can't get turned on."

Naturally, it will never be my fault even though I engineer it. The once regular orgasm becomes a stranger to our bedroom.

On other occasions, I will reinstate my masterful sexual technique and applying the lessons that I have learned so well I will take you along the road to heaven once again. After you have endured a barren period coupled with all the other hateful behaviours I have used against you, you will grasp this return to normal service with massive gratitude. The fuel flows and as I sense you nearing orgasm I will stop. The denial of sexual gratification will leave you frustrated, puzzled and hurt. Again, more fuel. It will prompt you to ask what is wrong and I will fabricate some reason as to why I had to stop. The addictive nature of the great sex that I once provided to you will raise its head again and you will want it so much, yet I exert my control over you by denying it. I may do this just for the sake of your reaction or I may do it to engineer you doing something for me with the promise of delivering. At the outset of our relationship if I had behaved this way you would have thought it most peculiar and probably lost interest in me or finished yourself off. Now during the devaluation, your confusion will lead you to think you have done something wrong. You will believe that you have done something to result in your being treated this way. It is puzzling for you and upsetting.

With regards to our orgasm, we will vacillate between two positions in order to further confuse and frustrate you. On the one hand, we will struggle to orgasm or even to get an erection. This is because now in the devaluation phase the true horror of the intimacy you want from sex is exposed. Previously we were able to deal with this when we were seducing you because of the positive fuel that we gathered. That has now gone and instead we are left with you craving intimacy through an act we have no interest in. This will disturb us and result in an in ability to achieve orgasm or even become aroused. You will try your best but our mind is not focussed on becoming physically stimulated by you. No, we are too busy enjoying your frustration and upset at this change of events. Once we seemed to have a near permanent erection and now it has vanished.

"This never happened with (previous girlfriend)"

"I guess I am just not as into you as I once thought."

"You are doing it all wrong, where did you learn to do this?"

"Good God your mouth is like a cheese grater, stop it."

"Just stop, nothing is happening; you just are not turning me on anymore."

We will layer this failure with such barbed comments because after all it is your fault. Do not dare to suggest that there is something wrong with us. Such a criticism will wound and ignite our fury and we will lash out at you. Of course, your dismay and disappointment will fuel us.

By contrast, on other occasions during the devaluation we will focus entirely on our orgasm to the detriment of yours. You are nothing more than an object in our sexual encounters anyway. Before, during the seduction, we dressed this up as something else with our flowery comments, noises of appreciation and enthusiastic declarations. Now all of that has been thrown to one side. We have no interest in maintaining that façade. You are expected to provide an orgasm no matter what and we will offer nothing in return. We will not touch you or caress you. We will issue commands to pleasure us when we see fit. We have discarded the alluring seduction we once applied to you when we coaxed you to use your hand on us under the table at a restaurant or fellate us in the cloakroom at a club. Now we demand you attend to us with your hand whilst we are driving. We deliberately drive faster to alarm you and urge you to get on with it and make us come. It is now exposed as the mechanical act it always was and it will disconcert you. We want you on your knees as you take us in your mouth and we will engage in making you gag, fucking your mouth and holding your head as we dominate you. You may as well be a fresh melon that we are plunging our cocks into. Again, the physical stimulation will bring us to climax but that is not what we are after. We want you to feel humiliated, used and degraded. We will insist on ejaculating over your face and into your hair. We want you to look up at us mouth open wide, submissive and waiting for our eruption. You may notice that there is a distinct preference for you only ever using your hand or mouth on us. This is because we regard your vagina as too intimate and we want to reinforce your status as an object by refraining from going there. There will be an insistence on anal sex and whereas once we may have attended to his in a consensual manner, getting you relaxed and ready, stimulated first with a lubricated digit before penetration, we will take it for granted that you agree and we will plunge away revelling in your gasps of pain as we penetrate you. We will insist on achieving climax and then berating you with comments such as:-

"That was a weak orgasm"

"I've had better."

"I had to think of your sister then so I could come."

"That was hard work."

"You are losing your touch."

There will not holding or tenderness like there once was. Previously we would achieve orgasm or more likely bring about yours and hold you afterwards telling you how beautiful you are and stroking you hair. We would make plans with you, pour our heart out for the future and say how much we loved you. Now we give you a scornful look before walking away to the shower or pulling our trousers on and making some excuse which requires us to leave. The dejection on your face fuels us and often we will hover outside the bedroom door waiting to hear your despairing sobs. You are completely bewildered as to how somebody could be so loving and deliver such delicious orgasms not that long ago who now has turned into a heartless and hurtful beast who is rough and uncaring on the few occasions that sex occurs. You dare not deny me when I come calling for sex and there are those of our number who will take it despite protest and objection since it is regarded as their right and entitlement. You are like a washing machine or television set. There to be used as and when we want it and we have on consideration for how you feel about it. If we had always been like this you might have some understanding (leaving aside the point that you would of course never have stayed with someone who behaved like this) but the sexual nirvana we gave you is such a stark contrast to the place where you are now that you are dumbstruck. Once in a while, the tender lovemaking will return and your delicious orgasm arrives with tears of joy and relief. The moment is fleeting for it will be snatched away again.

The orgasm was once something you treasured and relished. During devaluation, it is rarely delivered for you. During devaluation, it is used as a tool to frustrate, upset and humiliate you.

## Bondage

We may have introduced some light bondage during the seduction phase. You may already have engaged in it and regarded it as something pleasurable. You may have been curious and our caring and safe manner of introducing it persuaded you to allow us to tie you up. We made a show of discussing a safe word and ensuring you were not tied too tightly. We used silken scarves and behaved in a caring and erotic manner, which thrilled and delighted you. I never agreed to allow you to tie me up however. I regard this as ceding too much control and this is not permissible even in the seduction phase. I do know that there are members of our club who will allow this for the purpose of pleasing their partner in order to draw fuel from them. This usually happens with the Victim Variety of narcissist who is content to allow his partner to school him in this particular technique. They may engage in submissive behaviours through bondage (and other types of sexual behaviour) in order to experience that sense of being mothered by a dominating female. This provides fulfilment to the Victim Variety's partner and she provides fuel through her delight. He is then able to refuse to engage in such behaviour during the devaluation in order to gather an emotional response and the subsequent negative fuel.

In the instances where you might try and get us to submit to bondage when we find this offensive to our notion of superiority in such a situation we of course sweet-talked our way out of it happening by emphasising how we wanted to do it to you to heighten your sexual experience and intensify your orgasm and naturally you lapped all of this up. We are huge fans of bondage because we are wrapping you in isolation tape every day as part of our manipulation of you. Have a look at **The Devil's Toolkit** for more in that regard. Once we have you in the devaluation stage, we will use bondage in an oppressive manner. The silk scarves will have been put to one side and gaffer tape, rope and handcuffs will be used. Safe words will be ignored as we draw on the fear and hatred that emanate from you as you are subjugated. More often than not, we will actually use bondage as a way to frustrate you rather than subject you to actual physical harm. We will combine your bondage with denying your sexual gratification as we lead you towards satisfaction and then deny it you. We will also throw in some silent treatment by saying nothing and walking away from the bed or wherever we have you tied up your shouts or muffled cries if we have gagged you as well feeding us fuel. The sadistic of our brethren may subject you to caning for example whilst in such a helpless state as your pain-filled cries feed them fuel, but usually we are more interested in your humiliation, frustration and fear of seeing those handcuffs being taken from the bedside drawer. We may have engaged in just tying you to the bed during the seduction stage but then we transfer this to predicament bondage during devaluation. This may seem a subtle shift and as such will be in keeping with our salami-slicing technique, which we often apply when manipulating people. Predicament bondage lessens the positions you can adopt whilst bound and increases the sensation of pain. For instance, you may have to stand on your tiptoes for as long as you can bear it and in order to alleviate that pain, you lower your feet only for then to experience pain to your tied hair and nipples. The pain involved in this although not severe or of any long-term harm may be sufficient to draw a fuel-filled reaction from a partner unless of course it is actually something they enjoy. We will have been careful to ascertain that such an escalation is not something that you actually derive pleasure from as obviously this defeats the purpose of us doing this during devaluation. Bondage is a key method of devaluing you. We always regard you as being subjugated by us and dominating you in this fashion feeds our sense of power.

In order to avoid repetition it is worth pointing out that any form of sexual behaviour, which encapsulates a master and servant arrangement has the same considerations apply to it as they do as described with bondage. The Victim Variety of narcissist will willingly submit in order to further their desire to be mothered and in turn give their partner what they want so fuel is achieved. This will then be removed during the devaluation phase. Somatic and Elite narcissists are unlikely to submit to sexual practices whereby they are subjugated as this offends our concept of domination. Our conquest of you is what provides fuel. Our conquest may be by invitation and a friendly invasion if you will during seduction or a hostile takeover during devaluation but in either instance we are not willing participants in submissive behaviour. We will fulfil the dominant role and in our selection of victims, we will look for those who have empathic qualities who will subscribe to being treated in a submissive manner in the sexual arena. Accordingly, the behaviours described above which appertain to bondage are equal applicable to sexual scenarios involving discipline, punishment, smacking, caning, wax and edge play and so forth.

### **Incest**

Incest can occur as a consequence of fulfilling the fuel needs of a narcissist because engagement in this results in the opportunity to have sex with him or herself once again (in a manner similar to a homosexual experience) since the sex takes place with a genetic copy of the narcissist. During the seduction phase, the narcissist will engage in incest purely as a means to obtain positive fuel. The other party may be co-dependent and therefore willing to cross the barriers of something, which is regarded by society as taboo. The seduction of the other partner will be in the engaging and love bombing way that a non-related victim would be reeled in and therefore the related individual falls for the narcissist in the same way. Indeed, the narcissist is likely to be able to take advantage of a close relationship with a family member in order to achieve this goal of self-sex and obtain fuel.

In terms of the use of incest during devaluation, it is not so much a case of the devaluation occurring towards the related person (although this will inevitably happen when the supply of fuel is deemed defective) but rather that the occurrence of incest will be used to shock and morally outrage the non-related partner of the narcissist. The narcissist may engineer a situation of allowing the non-related partner to see a kiss on the mouth of the related partner, which lingers for too long in order to generate shock and an emotional reaction.

Alternatively the narcissist may admit to intense emotional affection which goes beyond that which is considered as normal, for the related individual or even confess to sexual fantasies about that person or go so far as to admit to sexual encounters with them. This is done purely as a method of triangulation with the non-related partner. This person will be deemed to be defective and that is why the narcissist has turned to the family member in this way. Not only is the non-related partner devalued by the infidelity they are also morally outraged by infidelity taking place within the context of an incestuous relationship. This double whammy results in the provision of high quality fuel for the narcissist when this is utilised in the devaluation phase.

## **Positioning**

We use this during our devaluation of you for the purposes of underlining that you are nothing other than an object to us. The manner of positioning can be done in several ways. Firstly, it will be by making you adopt various positions at our command. This is something that the somatic narcissist will particularly engage in.

"Lie there", "Bend over", "On your knees", "Not that way but this way" will be barked at you in order to bring about your compliance. You will feel like you are being bullied and ordered into various poses and positions at our behest. The loving and tender behaviour has been removed and instead you will be pushed, pulled and placed in certain positions. Secondly, it will be done by taking photographs of you. There will be none of the pseudo erotic photographer role-playing that we might have engaged in when we took photographs of you during the seduction stage. This will be more like appearing in a police line-up with orders and criticisms about the way you look and the poses you adopt. We treat you like a mannequin, adjusting you roughly and berating you if you do not hold the pose as we want. There is no aesthetic quality in what we are doing; it is purely a means of control and a method of drawing fuel from you, as you stand upset and bewildered. The third positioning is the most exhilarating for us when we have a range of bodies to position and direct. This occurs when we have coerced you or probably more accurately forced you to engage in group sex. We most likely will have recruited certain lieutenants to go along with this scenario or hired prostitutes in order to ensure that the other parties do not ally with you and defy us. We will take on the role of a director and experience considerable delight as we move limbs, position mouths and bottoms just where we want them to fulfil the masterpiece that we are creating in our minds. We feel like a god as we are able to position people and in turn, your involvement in this will make you feel small and unloved. Your subsequent reaction to this demeaning behaviour will result in the provision of fuel.

A further method of positioning which is beautifully combined with triangulation and in a strange way also with group sex is my scrapbook. I have a scrapbook into which I have pasted pictures of former girlfriends and sexual partners who I have photographed. I have also combined these pictures, all of which will be of these people in a naked state, with pictures of porn stars. Once I have pasted the pictures in I cut them up and place them into small boxes. One box contains heads, another arms, then legs, torsos, bottoms, breasts and private parts. I also have cut out the eyes and the hair so they have categories as well. I then like to arrange all these particular parts of people who I have bedded with those of the porn stars to create different women and ascribe names to them in my book. 'Firecrotch', 'Blowjob Queen', 'Flexible Friend', 'Stunning Trophy',' Dirty Whore' and such like. Like some beautiful versions of Dr Frankenstein's monster, I revel in my god-like ability to create these new ladies. The advantage is that only slight more than casual scrutiny will allow the viewer of this scrapbook to realise what I have done. I keep this hidden away during the seduction stage but once the devaluation has begun, I will happily leave it lying around for discovery or even allow myself to be caught masturbating whilst looking through this grimoire. The combination of being able to position these people as I might during group sex and then triangulate them with you results in a fantastic emotional response from and of course, the fuel that follows. I am careful to remove the book to another location once I have first used it to avoid any attempt by you to show it someone else or to destroy it even. Naturally, if you attempt to bring this book up in front of someone else or even when attacking me at a later date I will flatly deny its existence, accuse you of making things up and maintain that you are being hurtful in order to engender sympathy and further fuel. It is a masterful scheme, which I delight in using. I find considerable excitement from when I first photograph a new girlfriend during the seduction phase as I contemplate her eventual addition to the scrapbook. They really ought to be honoured that they are seen as fit to be included, rather than moaning about it.

## Strangers

The incessant march of the internet allows our kind more and more access to strangers. This increases the opportunities to extract fuel from these people. As I have explained in the fuel index, the fuel we obtain from strangers will be of the lowest grade in terms of proximity of supply. Strangers serve two purposes. The first is for a top up of fuel but the second and more pressing reason is to enable us to triangulate them with you. The preponderance of strangers in an online setting gives us opportunities to interact with them for the purposes of potentially promoting them within our fuel index and thus increasing the potency of the fuel that they might deliver to us. During devaluation you can expect strangers to feature more often (because we are using them more and also letting you be aware that we are using them more) in the following ways:-

- The use of dating sites to engage with and flirt with strangers

- The swapping of photographs with strangers via social media

- Use of chatrooms to interact with strangers

- Use of sex specific chatrooms to interact with strangers and discuss sexual matters

- Attending dogging sites to watch people have sex with strangers or to engage in sex acts with strangers

- Attendance at glory holes to engage in sex acts with strangers (more prevalent in the homosexual sphere)

- Involving a stranger in a threesome with you

- Meeting strangers for the purpose of sex

All of the above acts when linked with sex will provide a degree of fuel, albeit at a lower level, from the stranger but moreover it will provide material and opportunity to use that stranger for the purposes of triangulation.

**Humiliation**

There are many different sexual acts, which use the act of humiliation as the dynamic. If I dedicated a section to each of these various acts, the observations and commentary would become rather repetitive since the themes throughout them all will be the same. During devaluation, those sex acts, which have humiliation as a central dynamic, will be used against you *unless* we established in the seduction stage that you derive some enjoyment from this humiliation. We will then no longer provide that to you. If you do not then these wide range of sex acts containing humiliation will be used against you. This is to further objectify you, hurt you and as always ensure that you provide negative fuel. Which humiliation sex acts will we engage in. The following list contains examples but is by no means exhaustive:-

- Use of degrading names whilst engaged in sexual intercourse

- Forced repetition whereby you repeat the sexual command that has just been given to you

- Sexually disparaging comments about breast size, penis size, sexual performance

- Forced flattery whereby everything we do within the sexual union must be praised and confirmed as the right thing to do

- Spanking and caning

- Water sports including urinating on the other person

- Forced anal penetration using dildos and butt plugs

- Ejaculation on the face or hair

- Body worship for example having to kiss our feet

- Using you as a furniture, for example a foot stool

- Wearing a sign of ownership, for example a collar

- Forced masturbation

- Making you ask for permission to experience an orgasm

- Cuckolding

There is no sexual gratification at the heart of this humiliation for either party. If the narcissist happens to experience arousal or orgasm this is merely a by-product and was not something that was designed to happen. The above acts and many more besides are all about the narcissist exerting control over the victim, reinforcing our superior status and drawing fuel. Since we regard you as an appliance that is there to do as we say, your humiliation will come readily in the sexual arena. During the devaluation stage, we engage in your humiliation already in non-sexual ways such as:-

- Public humiliation by criticising you in front of others

- Micro-management by having you account for all and every action during your day

- Repeated criticism of you when alone with us

- Name-calling and blaming

With this background of mistreatment, it is a short step for the narcissist to transfer this behaviour and mind-set into the sexual arena. The intimate nature of these humiliations makes them far worse and will generate a more heightened emotional response from you with the subsequent provision of fuel.

## Pornography

Porn is a staple ingredient for us during the devaluation stage. We may have encouraged you to watch porn with us during the seduction stage in order to 'get you in the mood' but also to engender a sense of it being a task that we do together. During devaluation we will no longer watch porn with you, thus taking away something that you enjoyed doing with us and instead we commandeer it as our solo pursuit. The availability of on-line porn is heaven sent for us. As I have made mention the sexual act with you or anyone else is the equivalent of masturbating using someone else's body parts. If you asked most normal people whether they prefer to masturbate or engage in sexual activity with another person they would choose the latter. Ask us and we will say the former. This is because it uses less energy, allows us total control and moreover enables us to worship at the altar of self. Porn is the perfect vehicle for this. We will spend hours on-line looking through porn. Sometimes we may masturbate to it and other times we will not do so. By spending so much time watching other people engage in sexual acts we are reinforcing the fact that we would rather watch than do them with you. This belittles you. Furthermore, when we are watching porn we place ourselves inside the porn that we are watching. The sight of a buff and ripped man working his way through a succession of willing and vocal female participants is precisely how we regard our sexual performance. We are in effect watching ourselves perform and this pleases us. In the same way we regard our lives as a film with us as the star, watching porn has the same effect. We are in that movie showing all those women a fantastic time, exerting our sexual power over them. We will search through the internet to watch more and more bizarre pornography as we place ourselves inside each video in a position of dominance and power, or for the purposes of gaining ideas for our future interactions with you.

Alone in front a monitor or laptop we are able to sit as king in this sexual kingdom and become merged with the activities that we are watching. The knowledge we prefer this to you provides us with fuel, especially when you protest that we would rather sit all night in the study that go to bed with you. We will purposefully have a substantial pornography stash (downloaded movies, DVDs, magazines etc.) to boast to you about how extensive our appetite is for this material and also to humiliate you by showing our preference for this over you. Whilst we are able to control you during sex, both in the seduction and devaluation stages, we are in total and utter control when watching pornography and that appeals to our omnipotent and god-like sense.

The use of porn is also a place of retreat for us. As our interest in you has waned, we want to spend more time with the whores that we see on screen and porn facilitates this for us.

## Spontaneity

Whereas this will have once been the hallmark of our sexual engagements with you, embodying an anytime, anywhere, anyplace attitude to sex making it thrilling, we will during devaluation remove this. We will no longer surprise you and instead we will only engage in sex at certain set times, such as a Saturday morning or when you initiate it. If spontaneous sex was something we used regularly with you, you can expect that to vanish. This is to reinforce that you are no longer sexually special (not that you actually were of course) to us and that we regard sex as a chore with you (which is for once some actual truth). The main aim is to disappoint and frustrate so you react and we gain fuel.

## Public Sex

If we engaged in frequent acts of sex in public places in order to thrill and excite we will adopt the opposite stance during devaluation. We will refuse to engage in any public sex attempt should you initiate it. This is a typical behaviour of ours. Last week we liked it and this week we do not and there is no logical explanation for this. We liked steak yesterday but today we hate it and we will deny that we ever liked it. We will react with horror to any suggestion of engaging in public sex, labelling you a nymphomaniac and some kind of pervert. We will accuse you of trying to get us into trouble with the authorities and use this as an excuse to pick a fight with you. We will take this even further so that when we do engage in sexual activity with you we will only do it in the bedroom at home. We will make a great show of ensuring the curtains or blinds are closed, that the door is closed and possibly locked and that nobody can hear us, for example if there are adjoining neighbours or there are children in the house. This exaggerated response by seeking privacy is designed to confuse you after our sexual exhibitionism that we have shown previously.

**<u>Lighting</u>**

The compliments we have you about wanting to look at you whilst we made love and doing so with the right amount of sympathetic lighting are now forgotten. During devaluation, we want to maintain that we never did this and in order to heighten your confusion and hurt we will adopt a completely different stance. We will insist on bright lights during sex so it feels like you are lying underneath the floodlights and this will make you feel uncomfortable. Everything will be highlighted and any insecurity you may have about your body and looks will be accentuated. We do not care about that and as for ourselves; well we look great in any light don't we? Alternatively, we will only engage in sexual acts with you in complete darkness. This will be done prompt a reaction from you both before and after by insisting that any sexual activity occurs cloaked in darkness.

## Picture and Films

During devaluation, this category within the sexual sphere is used in two ways. The first is that the material we have obtained from you consensually during the seduction stage will be broadcast. You will find your pictures scattered across social media, chat rooms and porn sites and your videos uploaded to as many sites as possible. We will often do this without telling you allowing it to be a delicious bomb that will explode sometime in the future. Alternatively, we will distribute it or threaten to do so, near the time of our discard of you as a final kiss-off and a last gathering of delicious fuel. This act nowadays goes by the label of revenge porn. We have no difficulty if we are identified in the material because we are content for people to see how good we are at sex. We also have no concern for the consequences of this action because you agreed to be filmed and therefore in our minds we are entitled to distribute this material as we see fit.

The other use of film and photographs during devaluation is to take a record of the degrading and humiliating sex acts that we put you through. We will keep these to use for our own viewing pleasure as part of our expansive porn collection. We will threaten to release this material in order to maintain control over you and draw a reaction. The fact we set up a camera on a tripod whilst engaging in these acts of sexual devaluation also draws further fuel from you.

## Broadcasting

We loved to tell the world how wonderful our sex life was with you. Once we enter the devaluation stage this broadcasting of 'good' news will end. We either call a halt to it completely no longer explaining how you satisfy us and provide us with great sex so that the information gets back to you, or we will begin to circulate negative information about you. We will ensure our lieutenants are engaged in circulating this information on our behalf and also to ensure you get to hear about it. The information will be hurtful for example accusing you of frigidity, mocking your sexual competence and the like. We may disseminate information about things you have done which would viewed poorly by other people and we will often look to ensure that information about your slutty behaviour ends up in the ears of people such as your family or employer for maximum effect. Having your sexual vulnerabilities and behaviours broadcast around town will prove especially hurtful and is often used as parting shot as we discard you.

## Sexual Past

This will also be used in broadcasting. If we are able to learn, something about your sexual past which is embarrassing or hurtful we will be supportive and understanding at first. We will then look to exploit this knowledge against you during devaluation. We might reveal a particular sexual mishap that you suffered or some particular hang up that you have in the bedroom. The female of our kind will revel in using any kind of sexual dysfunction such as premature ejaculation and/or impotence against their male victims. We will also use this information within our relationship to extract fuel from you. You will recall my example of a former girlfriend Sam and her eventual admission about the abuse she suffered at the hands of her uncle's friend at the allotments which she otherwise loved attending. Once I entered the devaluation stage with Sam, I used this against her. I would detour past a set of allotments (it did not even have to be the same allotments) and suggest that we pop in for some al fresco and spontaneous sex amidst the plants. I did not even have to get her to leave the care to garner an emotional reaction from her at the suggestion of revisiting any kind of sexual behaviour in that setting. She would burst into tears and plead not to go. I toyed with dragging her into one set of allotments once but the noise she was making inside the car would easily have alerted people nearby and would have made execution of the plan very difficult. It was enough to generate the reaction inside the car and the fuel that followed. Our kind will always learn about your sexual past and find a way of using that information against you by twisting it and using it against you.

## **Contraception**

During devaluation, we will insist on contraception being used even though we had a laissez-faire attitude to it beforehand. We will not trust you to address contraception even though we will insist you do. You may want to try for a child and irrespective of whether we have already children together or not (this does not enter into our thinking) we will not grant you this wish. We will keep a separate stash of contraceptives available (since we will accuse you of trying to sabotage them) and make a great show of using them.

## **Sex Drive**

The once rampant sex drive will dwindle to next to nothing and only be used out of an occasional sense of obligation (cerebral) or for the purposes of gathering fuel by engaging in devaluing sexual acts with you (somatic or elite). This will be done to appeal to your sense of healing and fixing, as you will try and initiate sex with us. We will be obtaining sex from an alternative source at this point and we will use this supposedly dwindling sex drive as evidence of how you no longer attract us. We will naturally blame you and couple this diminution with insults aimed at your appearance, technique and behaviour. You will do plenty to try to revive our dwindling interest. We will also combine this with watching plenty of porn and ensuring you know we are doing this. We will explain we have no interest in you to triangulate you with the porn we are watching. We may express we have no interest in sex at all but then be caught indulging in porn in order to contradict our stated position. As ever this is all done to confuse you and draw a reaction.

## **Tenderness**

This will be removed from all sexual engagements with us once the devaluation phase has been embarked on. This ensures you fall hard and fast as you lose that wonderful sensation of being held, loved and cared for. Instead, it will be replaced with coldness, an authoritarian approach to sex and treating you like the meat puppet we truly regard you as. Whereas we once caressed you, we will slap your bottom and hard, we will push and pull, flipping you over as we revel in our sexual control over you. You will feel like you have been placed in a tumble dryer and once we have achieved our goal, you will be left crumpled, tossed away like a rag after we have had our fill. That once gentle and tender person becomes a distant memory (although of course he will be reinstated from time to time as part of a mini-Hoover in order to further your addiction to us and confuse you) and instead an unfeeling ogre will have taken his place.

## **New Sex Acts**

Variety was once the spice of our sex life together. We carefully introduced new and exciting techniques and activities into our sex life and you readily embraced them. Once we devalue, we will:-

- Claim we no longer like or even liked those acts. We will look at you aghast if you try to perform them with us;

- Remove all variety and return to vanilla sex or just focus on those sex acts we know you do not like and repeatedly perform those.

Accordingly, if there is anything in the sexual arena that we once did that you enjoyed we will either remove it or do the opposite in order to confuse and upset you.

## Voyeurism

This has been touched on in some of the categories above. We will engage in voyeurism during devaluation as this allows us to survey the unfolding sexual tapestry in front of us. As I explained in our use of porn, we will place ourselves in the position of directing the action. We will enjoy watching other people have sex either through peeping through someone's window or at dogging sites for example. We will attend sex shows in order to settle back and watch the action. In our minds, this is all being acted out for us alone and we will feel a reinforcement of our omnipotence by engaging in this. It also allows us to freeze you out of our sexual experiences and triangulate them with you. We will express a clear preference for engaging in this because we regard it as akin to a god watching the world as it goes about its business beneath him. It is worth mentioning that the way society is now it lends itself to voyeurism. As I have written before about how the world is creating more of our kind, the world is also a much more voyeuristic place. Reality television is the prime exponent of this. We want to be the fly on the wall seeing how other people's lives unfold for us to laud or criticise them. We need to see how the other half live, be they somehow "better" or "beneath" us. We want to know what people are doing, where and when. Social media encourages this by enabling people to ascertain where someone else currently is and what they are doing. We embrace this in a general sense as it allows us to maintain and create connections by the assimilation of information in this way. In a sexual sense, we enjoy conserving our energy, looking on as we perhaps masturbate and imagining ourselves in the sexual scene that is taking place before us. If we are not envisaging ourselves as part of it we are revelling in the fact that these people are doing this solely for our benefit as they wish to impress us. Whatever our reasoning the message is clear to you; you are not involved and you are not wanted.

## Madonna/Whore Complex

Essentially, those of our kind who have this complex desire a sexual partner who we consider degraded and exciting (the whore) and by contrast we cannot desire the respected partner (the Madonna). In my experience however, I suggest that it goes further than this and in some instances, it follows three stages:-

- The 'good' whore;

- The 'bad' whore ; and

- The Madonna

We categorise you from the moment that we meet. Initially we will regard you as a good whore because you create a sexual interest in us. You are there to be conquered and in effect, you are challenging us. This sense of you being denied to us spurs us on and encourages us to use our repertoire of love-bombing techniques against you. During this period, the sexual element will be exciting and desirable. This is because you remain new and interesting. You are like an inviting whore who has all manner of new and alluring things to offer us. This holds our attention and we want to make you ours. We do not want to purchase you but rather we want to use our skills and charm to cause you to give us fuel freely. The whore sells. We want you to give it for free and this is intensely exciting and interesting for us.

It is because we are still conquering you. You may tell us how much you love and adore you but we are still marching through your territory, causing you to cede land to us. We invade your friendships and take them over, controlling how you deal with your friends. We manage your career for you. We park our tanks on the lawn of your finances. We occupy your time. We continue with this blitzkrieg as we advance into all areas of your life, overcoming any resistance (if there is any) swiftly with our regiments of love-troopers, battalions of compliments and brigades of grand gestures. No part of your life is left alone and especially not the sexual element. As we ensure you fall deeper and deeper in love and dependency with us, we are surging deep into your sexual psyche. We are knocking down barriers as we engage in additional and new sexual experiences with you. We dominate your sex life as we have sex with you repeatedly. This invasion takes place over time and during this stage, although we may regard you as a princess and tell you this we actually consider you a whore. We will treat you favourably and with love and affection, which may seem strange if we consider you as whore, yet just because someone is given the label of whore it does not mean that we cannot be pleasant and loving to them and especially if this is all part of our invasion and you are giving us fuel. The description of whore actually means that you are exciting in our eyes. You are a good whore because we have an interest in you and you are providing us with positive fuel. We love everything about you because it is fresh and new and especially in a sexual sense. The fuel that flows from our sexual union is potent indeed. A normal person may find sex with a whore exciting because it is still regarded as taboo thing to do, it may be extra marital and the opportunity to do certain acts with this whore that the normal person cannot ordinarily do provides that frisson of excitement. That new quality is the same for us and that is why we regard you as a whore during this seduction phase.

When devaluation occurs, dependent on the type of narcissist that we are, we may move to a bad whore phase and then onto the Madonna or go straight to the Madonna stage. In the latter instance, you have lost our interest in a sexual sense but we still want the mothering, caring side that you provide for us. The step from good whore to Madonna is most prevalent with the Victim Variety of narcissist and the cerebral narcissist because sex does not play a huge part in those relationships. The Victim Variety especially craves the nurturing and mothering above all else. Having used his lack of sexual desire and/or sexual incompetence as a method of seducing the mothering empath he can now jettison the sexual element and focus entirely on receiving the nurturing element by regarding her as his Madonna. He will be working on a new prospect at the same time by luring in the good whore (who is especially good in the Victim Variety's eyes as she is helping him overcome his sexual deficiencies).

The somatic or elite narcissist will still have an interest in using sex to gather fuel and is not ready to place their victim in the position of being a Madonna yet. There is a further stage for this victim and that is of bad whore. In this position, she remains exciting to us and retains that whorish quality because the provision of fuel will now be of a negative variety. This is when the degrading and humiliating acts are meted out against this victim in the same way that a person may feel they cannot do such things with their wife but they can with a faceless whore. The somatic or elite narcissist cannot go straight to the Madonna stage as there are masses of valuable fuel to obtain and this is obtained still in the sexual arena. It is however harvested through the application of devaluing techniques with the kind, loving and attentive façade stripped away. The victim finds herself treated like a street whore, debased and degraded as the narcissist extracts the negative fuel.

Whilst this is ongoing, a new good whore will have been sourced and they are used as the focus of our seduction just as you once were. As we lose interest in your sexually, you then become the Madonna. You will continue to want to make us feel loved, cared for and happy despite the way we have treated you. This happens because you are innately built this way but also because we have conditioned you in this manner as you fight to reclaim the golden period. Once you are the Madonna we will no longer be interested in even trying to secure negative fuel from you in a sexual sense and you may also be close to discard if we are of the somatic or elite variety. We will draw fuel from you by continuing our devaluation of you whilst taking from you the care and love you continue to give. You are considered saintly for doing this in our minds.

In essence, when we first encounter you, no matter how much we may elevate you and use words and gestures to that effect, we regard you as a good whore. We see you as something to use sexually to gain fuel. We will treat you in a kind and loving fashion because at this stage, this is what you want and we must do this in order to draw you into our sphere of influence and also to cause you to churn out fuel. It does not however stop our view of you as a whore.

Once devaluation commences some of our partners become Madonnas very quickly as there is a complete withdrawal of any sexual union. You become sexless to us and there is no interest in your sexually any more.

The whorish excitement has evaporated. We will find another whore to provide this for us and/or utilise the many whores we see in pornography since each new webpage is fresh and exciting in the same way you once were. With other victims, you will become bad whores from whom we can extract negative fuel as we subject you to degrading and unpleasant devaluing behaviours.

The devaluation period is an unpleasant one for our victims anyway. The use of sex when we devalue, because it is so intimate and owing to your binding of love and sex together, means that its impact is devastating on you but it also means we extract significant and potent negative fuel from you.

# Sex and the Grand Hoover

Every time that I looked at this heading in my notes it put me in mind of the urban myth about the gentleman who is admitted to his local hospital with his member firmly wedged in the hose attachment of a Hoover. When asked by the amused junior doctor how he came to be in this position he explained that he had been doing some spring cleaning whilst naked and slipped with the unfortunate consequence that his pride and joy became stuck in the hose attachment. More likely, he was a narcissist engaging in some autoeroticism. With that anecdote out of the way, we now turn to how we use sex in the Hoover stage.

During devaluation, we operate a policy of push and pull. We will repeatedly subject you to confusing and belittling behaviour as we cause you to provide us with negative fuel. In order to keep you a short respite is granted from this and/or to avoid the risk of you leaving us if we push this abusive behaviour too far. We perform if you will a mini-Hoover by allowing you access to the illusion we created that forms the golden period. Relieved and elated you pour fresh positive fuel over us and you also convince yourself that you have succeeded in getting the 'old' we back. You will then be pushed away again as the devaluation continues and you will remain transfixed as you try to return to the golden period. We will use sex during these mini-Hoovers, as we shall when we Grand Hoover you on a larger scale and therefore the comments and observations below fall equally to be applied to the mini-Hoover as they do the larger scale Hoover.

We will eventually discard you after a period of devaluation. There is no set period for the duration of our devaluation of you before the discard occurs. There are several factors, which influence it including:-

- The level and quality of fuel you have been providing us of a negative nature

- The other sources of fuel that we obtain from our other appliances and in particular the new prime source of supply

- Whether you break free of our grip

- External factors such as illness or moving away which affect our ability to draw fuel from you

However, the cessation in our relationship has come about there will be a Grand Hoover. It may be within hours of you trying to end the relationship or it may be a decade after we vanished into the mist one evening never to be seen again. The reasons behind the duration of the hiatus are not necessary for the purpose of this book and will be addressed in a forthcoming publication dedicated to the art of the Hoover. There are two reasons why we engage in the Grand Hoover:-

- To gain fuel from the Grand Hoover itself ; and

- To gain fuel by reactivating your pipeline to us.

The fuel that we derive from Hoovering anybody is sweet and potent but it as it most potent when we gather this fuel from a former intimate partner who is expressing their relief that we are together and those tears of joy are trickling down those cheeks just as we remember. This gives us the ultimate fuel. Why is that?

- You tried to escape but we pulled you back in. That shows how magnetic and powerful we are;

- We cast you aside after abusing you terribly and despite this, we pulled you back in. This shows our magnetism and power once again;

- The expression of relief through words and tears are at the top end of method of delivery of fuel;

- We know we will be getting more fuel from you;

- It sends a powerful message to those traitors who may have helped you leave us/warned you not to go back that we are the kings

- It underlines how superior we are. No mere normal individual can wield such power over another person

- We can triangulate you with the person we replaced you with

Accordingly, the Grand Hoover is probably the most important manoeuvre that we make. Seduction provides rewards as does devaluation but the Hoover stands above those two stages. Once we have Hoovered you, we have in fact performed a seduction once again but it has to be done in a different way because you may have increased wariness and resistance to our wiles. We will allow a golden period to happen once again following a Grand Hoover and this golden period may last for a reasonable period of time, weeks and possibly a few months. It will certainly last longer than the golden period which follows a mini-Hoover. Once the same problems arise in this second golden period as the first then the devaluation will begin again.

How then do we use sex in the Grand Hoover? We essentially provide you with the same sexual attention approach and outcome as we did when we first engaged in our seduction of you. You will be aware from your own experience and/or reading the chapter on seduction above how powerful that sexual encounter is. Few can resist it the first time de deploy our sexual charm to ensnare you and when it comes to the Hoover we have specifically ensured that our prospects of a successful Hoover will be maximised through our use of sex. The reasons for this are as follows:-

- We have made you addicted to the sex that we gave you. You will be craving this sex once again because of your addiction to it. Deprived of this sex and in circumstances which you will have found traumatic the promise of its reinstatement is a powerful incentive;

- Your indoctrination in the concept of lovesex means that the binding of love and sex together proves difficult to resist to your empathic nature;

- You have been depleted of your coping mechanisms, self-esteem, self-worth, critical thinking and resistance. This means trying to resist our sexual overture during the Grand Hoover (even if you wanted to) becomes difficult;

- The position you find yourself in (whether you choose to escape or whether we discarded you) means you feel low and dejected. The prospect of feeling better through enjoying sex with us proves irresistible. Like the alcoholic who requires just one more drink the temptation of feeling euphoric again, even if warning bells are ringing is very difficult to resist;

- You have seen that we coupled with someone new. No matter how illogical it may appear to want to be with someone who has treated you so badly, the way we have conditioned you means you cannot stand to think that we might be happy with someone else or they are making us happy or that they are receiving that perfect and delicious sexual experience from us. You want us back.

All of these factors mean that we are pushing on an open door. We will blitzkrieg you in our attempt to perform this Grand Hoover because we want that potent fuel. We will of course be applying all manner of manipulative techniques as well as those of a sexual nature to Grand Hoover you. Those additional techniques and methods are detailed in **Escape: How to Beat the Narcissist** and **Departure Imminent: Preparing for No Contact to Beat the** Narcissist. Those methods are powerful in themselves and even more so when sex is added to the mix. We will make every effort to impress to get you back within our sphere of influence and we use sex as central part of this Grand Hoover. What can you expect then when we use sex in this Grand Hoover? The following is likely to happen:-

- We will telephone you and remind you of the times we used to turn you on with our seductive conversations down the telephone line;

- We will bombard you with e-mails and text messages making reference to the unparalleled sex that we enjoyed together and reminding you of how compatible we are together and how we can do this again;

- We will pour scorn on the person we are currently with by saying they do not come close to providing us with the sexual nirvana you gave us;

- We will send you pictures of our honed and chiselled physique if we are of the somatic or elite narcissistic variety

- We will say that nobody helped us with our sexual dysfunction and overcoming our inhibitions if we are of the Victim Variety

- We will send you a copy of any erotic film we made together with associated compliments and pleading. Any material that we compiled during the devaluation will not be provided and instead we shall rely on the tender and beautiful material created during the seduction

- We will enlist our Lieutenants to remind you how sexually compatible we are together and how we apparently talk of little else about how you were the best sexual partner we ever had

- We will turn up at your home, office of other places we know you will be in order to try to kiss you and begin to initiate sex with you again. We have no qualms about doing this in public places because we are not worried about what others think; besides their reactions will only give us fuel in any event. Moreover, if there is the sweetest fuel available up for grabs this is hardly an inconvenience to us.

- We will ask for one last time in bed with you under the auspices of "seeking closure" or "having something to remember during the long, dark nights". It is all a fabrication designed to allow us to bring our sexual proficiency to bear. Believe me, if you let us into your bed, it will not be the last time. Once you have tasted this sexual delight, once again it is just like an addict shooting up with heroin. The relief, delight and pleasure is so overwhelming (when combined with feeding your addiction and staving off the misery) that you will want it again and we will end up staying the whole night as we wrap ourselves together.

A Grand Hoover is extremely hard to resist at the best of times and when we use sex in our methodology, you face a huge battle to resist us. This is no idle boast. I have done this many, many times. The groundwork that has been done during the seduction phase, the misery of the devaluation phase and now the promise of a return to the promised land proves very hard to resist. Sex is the key to opening your defensive gates and we will use it every single time we perform the Grand Hoover if we are of the somatic and elite varieties of narcissist.

# Conclusion

Sex is an all-pervasive weapon of the narcissist. Since sex is everywhere, we tap into this to achieve the omnipotence for which we are known. Sex is important in many different ways to people and especially those who are conditioned in the way that love is generally regarded by society. To us sex is just a tool. It is a device, which shifts and alters as we seek to exert our influence over you and draw fuel from you. Sex will seduce you, sex will hurt you and sex will bring you back to us. More often than not, when you think back to your time with a narcissist you will immediately recall how wonderful and mind blowing the sex was. Sex was used to lift you up and then cast you down. We used it smooth things over, halt arguments and get our way. The provision of brilliant sex was invariably the marker of the golden period. We might have been shouting at you and degrading you yet with one swift volte-face we push you onto the bed and deliver that amazing hit of sexual excellence and you are putty in our hands once again.

Our sexual appetites vary dependent on the type of narcissist that we are. We engage in bizarre sexual activities but that is only a way to get to our fuel. Some of our kind engages in the immoral, the hurtful and even the illegal but these are all because sex is the super highway that leads to vast deposits of fuel. There is nothing else like sex for enabling us to achieve our goals of acquiring fuel. Sex links everything up for us. It connects seduction with devaluation with hoovering. Our triumvirate of manipulation is accentuated, accelerated and heightened by the application of sex. You now have a greater understanding of how sex and the narcissist operate and most importantly how this involves you. You may find some of our behaviours distasteful but is that really something you did not expect? You may find some of our reasoning strange but you will be used to that by now. Most of all you will now understand just how powerful sex is in the narcissist's hands. Or mouth. Or between his legs. What now for me? Time for bed. Care to join me?

* * * * * * * *

# Further reading from H G Tudor

Evil

Narcissist: Seduction

Narcissist: Ensnared

Manipulated

Confessions of a Narcissist

More Confessions of a Narcissist

Further Confessions of a Narcissist

From the Mouth of a Narcissist

Escape: How to Beat the Narcissist

Danger: 50 Things You Should Not Do With a Narcissist

Departure Imminent: Preparing for No Contact to beat the Narcissist

Fuel

Chained: The Narcissist's Co-Dependent

A Delinquent Mind

Fury

Beautiful and Barbaric

The Devil's Toolkit

# Further interaction with H G Tudor

## Knowing the Narcissist

@narcissist_me

Facebook

Narcsite.wordpress.com

Made in the USA
Columbia, SC
14 January 2019